I0013541

Surviving AI Job Displacement

High Paying Jobs and Skills to Thrive
in an AI Driven World, Focusing on AI
Resistant Careers and Essential Training
for Job Security

Hunter Hazelton

Life Level Up Books

Contents

AI Today and Tomorrow

Artificial Intelligence (AI) has become an integral part of our daily lives, changing the way we interact with technology and make decisions. This section explores what AI can do today, including its uses in everyday life and how it affects decision-making processes.

Overview of Current AI Capabilities

AI technology has advanced to a point where it can handle large amounts of data, identify patterns, and carry out tasks with impressive precision. Here are some key abilities:

- **Natural Language Processing (NLP):** Enables machines to understand and generate human language.

- **Computer Vision:** Allows machines to interpret and make decisions based on visual data.

- **Predictive Analytics:** Uses statistical algorithms and machine learning techniques to identify future outcomes based on historical data.

- **Automation:** Facilitates the performance of repetitive tasks without human intervention.

These capabilities have been integrated into various fields, revolutionizing how tasks are performed and offering greater efficiency and accuracy.

Examples of AI in Daily Routines

AI applications subtly but significantly impact our daily lives. Here are some examples:

- **Voice Assistants:** Devices like Amazon's Alexa or Apple's Siri use NLP to understand commands, set reminders, play music, and control smart home devices.

- **Recommendation Systems:** Platforms such as Netflix and Spotify employ predictive analytics to suggest movies or songs based on user preferences.

- **Navigation Apps:** Google Maps utilizes AI to provide real-time traffic updates and optimal routes.

- **Smart Home Devices:** Thermostats like Nest learn from user behaviors to adjust heating and cooling for energy efficiency.

These instances demonstrate how AI seamlessly integrates into our everyday activities, enhancing convenience and personalization.

How AI Influences Decision-Making Processes

AI's ability to analyze large datasets and extract insights greatly impacts decision-making processes in various industries:

1. **Healthcare:** AI assists doctors in diagnosing diseases by analyzing medical images with higher accuracy than traditional methods. For example, IBM Watson Health is known for its diagnostic prowess in oncology.

2. **Finance:** Algorithms determine trading strategies by analyzing market trends, thereby optimizing investment portfolios. Companies like BlackRock utilize AI for risk management and financial planning.

3. **Retail:** Businesses use AI to predict inventory needs based on consumer behavior patterns, reducing wastage and improving supply chain efficiency.

4. **Human Resources:** AI-driven tools assist in candidate screening by evaluating resumes against job requirements, thus speeding up the recruitment process.

The ability of AI to process information rapidly and accurately offers a competitive edge by enabling informed decisions based on real-time data.

Machine Learning and Deep Learning: The Core of AI

Machine learning and **deep learning** are the main technologies behind modern artificial intelligence. It's important to understand what they are and how they differ in order to appreciate their real-world uses.

Definition and Differences

Machine Learning (ML)

- A type of AI that trains algorithms to get better at a task through experience.

- Uses structured data to find patterns, make predictions, and automate decisions.

- Examples: recommendation systems on Netflix and Spotify that suggest content based on user behavior.

Deep Learning (DL)

- A specialized form of ML that uses complex neural networks with multiple layers to analyze different types of data.

- Can work with unstructured data like images, audio, and text.

- Examples: facial recognition systems and language translation services like Google Translate.

The main difference between the two is their complexity and capability. While machine learning can handle simpler tasks using basic algorithms, deep learning is better suited for more complex scenarios that require analyzing high-dimensional data.

Real-World Applications

Both technologies have made their way into many fields, improving functionality and intelligence in ways never seen before:

Healthcare

- ML algorithms predict disease outbreaks by analyzing patient records and public health data.

- DL models assist radiologists by identifying anomalies in medical imaging, such as tumors.

Finance

- Banks use ML for fraud detection by monitoring transaction patterns.

- DL helps in high-frequency trading where decisions are made in nanoseconds based on vast datasets.

Autonomous Vehicles

- ML enables self-driving cars to make real-time decisions using sensor data.

- DL processes visual information from cameras to detect objects and navigate traffic safely.

The Role of Data

Data is crucial for both machine learning and deep learning models. The quality, quantity, and diversity of data directly affect how well these algorithms perform:

1. Data Collection

- Gathering relevant datasets from various sources like IoT devices, social media, and transactional systems.

- Considering ethical issues when collecting data to avoid invading people's privacy.

2. Data Preprocessing

- Cleaning up the data to remove any noise or errors that could distort results.

- Normalizing or scaling features so they all contribute equally during model training.

3. Model Training

- Using past data to teach algorithms how to recognize patterns or predict outcomes.

- Fine-tuning model parameters repeatedly to improve accuracy while preventing overfitting.

4. Validation & Testing

- Dividing the data into training, validation, and test sets for thorough model evaluation.

- Using cross-validation techniques for better generalization performance.

In simple terms, machine learning is like a skilled craftsman who creates intelligent solutions from structured datasets, while deep learning is like a master artist who understands complex patterns within unstructured information. Both need a lot of high-quality data to work effectively. This close relationship between algorithms and datasets shows the transformative power that can be achieved by integrating them into our everyday technologies.

Natural Language Processing: AI Understanding Human Language

What is NLP and Why Does It Matter?

Natural language processing (NLP) is a field at the intersection of artificial intelligence and linguistics. It enables computers to understand, interpret, and generate human language. This technology allows machines to bridge the gap between human communication and digital data, making it a cornerstone of modern AI applications.

Why is NLP Important?

NLP plays a crucial role in various aspects of technology and society:

- **Improved User Experience:** By understanding user input more naturally, NLP makes interactions with technology smoother.

- **Data Analysis:** NLP can process large amounts of text data for tasks like sentiment analysis or topic classification.

- **Automation:** Tasks such as translation, summarization, and report generation become easier with NLP.

How is NLP Used in Real Life?

NLP has numerous applications that impact our daily lives:

Chatbots

One of the most visible uses of NLP is in chatbots. These virtual assistants can have conversations that feel human-like to provide customer service, answer questions, or even give personalized recommendations. For example:

- **Customer Support:** Companies like Amazon use chatbots to handle millions of customer inquiries every day.

- **Personal Assistants:** Siri and Alexa use NLP to understand voice commands and perform tasks like setting reminders or playing music.

Text Analysis

NLP isn't just about conversations; it also helps analyze text data:

- **Sentiment Analysis:** Businesses keep an eye on social media to understand how customers feel about their products.

- **Content Moderation:** Platforms like Facebook use NLP to automatically find and filter inappropriate content.

What Challenges Does NLP Face?

While NLP has great potential, creating effective systems comes with challenges:

1. **Ambiguity:** Human language can be unclear. Words might mean different things based on context. For instance, "bank" could refer to a financial institution or the side of a river.

2. **Understanding Context:** It's tough for machines to grasp the bigger picture in a conversation. They often struggle with things like sarcasm or implied meanings.

3. **Multiple Languages:** Building models that can understand and produce multiple languages needs a lot of computing power and diverse training data.

4. **Avoiding Bias:** Making sure AI systems don't reinforce biases found in training data is an important ethical issue.

How Can We Tackle These Challenges?

To overcome these obstacles, we need:

- Advanced algorithms that better capture context

- Diverse datasets representing different language nuances

- Ethical guidelines steering the development process

Examples Highlighting These Challenges

Real-life examples make these challenges clearer:

> "GPT-3's performance has shown incredible improvements yet reveals limitations in understanding complex contexts or ethical considerations."

Developers are always working on improving these systems to better handle the intricacies of human language.

Understanding how natural language processing fits into everyday technologies shows us just how much AI influences our lives.

Computer Vision: How AI Sees the World

Computer vision is a branch of artificial intelligence that enables machines to interpret and make decisions based on visual data. By mimicking human vision, computer vision systems aim to understand images and videos at a level of detail comparable to human comprehension. This capability is crucial in various domains where visual information plays a pivotal role.

Definition and Importance of Computer Vision

Computer vision involves the development of algorithms that can process, analyze, and understand visual data from the world. It harnesses techniques from machine learning and deep learning to enable computers to recognize patterns, classify objects, and extract meaningful insights from images.

Importance:

- **Enhanced Accuracy**: Machines can process vast amounts of visual data more quickly and accurately than humans.

- **Automation**: Enables automation in tasks that were previously manual, such as quality inspection in manufacturing.

- **Scalability**: Applicable across numerous industries, leading to innovations in solutions and services.

Applications in Various Fields

The applications of computer vision span multiple sectors:

1. Security

Surveillance: Automated image recognition systems monitor public spaces for suspicious activities or unauthorized access.

Facial Recognition: Used by law enforcement agencies for identifying individuals in crowds or verifying identities at checkpoints.

2. Healthcare

Medical Imaging: Enhances diagnostic accuracy by analyzing X-rays, MRIs, and CT scans to detect anomalies such as tumors or fractures.

Surgical Assistance: Augmented reality (AR) guides surgeons with real-time imaging overlays during complex procedures.

3. Retail

Inventory Management: Uses image recognition to keep track of stock levels on shelves.

Customer Experience: AI-powered cameras analyze customer behavior and preferences to tailor marketing strategies.

4. Autonomous Vehicles

Navigation: Self-driving cars utilize computer vision to recognize traffic signs, pedestrians, and other vehicles for safe navigation.

Accident Prevention: Real-time analysis of road conditions helps prevent collisions by taking preemptive actions.

Limitations and Ongoing Research

Despite its advancements, computer vision faces several challenges:

- **Complexity of Visual Data**: Real-world environments are dynamic and unpredictable, making it difficult for AI systems to interpret all scenarios accurately.

- **Data Quality**: High-quality labeled datasets are essential for training robust models, yet obtaining these datasets can be resource-intensive.

- **Ethical Implications**: Issues such as privacy invasion

through surveillance systems raise ethical concerns about the deployment of computer vision technologies.

Ongoing research aims to address these limitations by exploring:

- **Improved Algorithms**: Developing more sophisticated models that can handle diverse and complex visual inputs efficiently.

- **Synthetic Data Generation**: Using synthetic data to augment real-world datasets, thereby reducing the dependency on extensive labeled data.

- **Ethical Frameworks**: Establishing guidelines for ethical use that balance innovation with respect for individual rights.

The interplay between advancing technologies and addressing inherent challenges propels the field forward. The potential impact on numerous aspects of daily life is profound, reflecting both the promise and responsibility that comes with these innovations.

AI in Healthcare: Diagnostics, Treatment, and Beyond

Role of AI in Improving Diagnostics Accuracy

Artificial Intelligence (AI) is changing the healthcare industry by making diagnoses more accurate. Traditional diagnostic methods often depend on human expertise, which can be prone to mistakes and limitations. AI systems, however, use large amounts of data and complex algorithms to find patterns that even the most skilled doctors might miss. Here are some examples:

- **Radiology**: AI algorithms analyze medical images such as X-rays, MRIs, and CT scans to detect anomalies like tumors or fractures with remarkable precision.

- **Pathology**: Machine learning models assist pathologists in examining tissue samples, identifying cancerous cells faster and more accurately than manual methods.

- **Cardiology**: AI-powered tools interpret electrocardiograms (ECGs) and echocardiograms to diagnose heart conditions early.

By reducing diagnostic errors, AI not only improves patient outcomes but also eases the workload on healthcare professionals.

Personalized Medicine Through AI Algorithms

Personalized medicine tailors treatment plans to individual patient characteristics, a concept that has gained traction with the advent of AI. Unlike traditional one-size-fits-all approaches, personalized medicine considers genetic, environmental, and lifestyle factors. Here's how AI contributes:

1. **Genomic Analysis**: AI algorithms analyze genetic data to predict susceptibility to diseases and response to treatments. Companies like 23andMe use machine learning techniques to provide insights into individual health risks based on genetic makeup.

2. **Drug Discovery**: Machine learning accelerates drug discov-

ery by predicting which compounds will be effective against specific targets. This reduces time and costs associated with bringing new drugs to market.

3. **Treatment Optimization**: AI can recommend optimal treatment plans by analyzing patient data alongside clinical guidelines. IBM's Watson for Oncology, for example, provides evidence-based treatment options tailored to each patient's unique profile.

Through these applications, AI enables more precise and effective healthcare interventions.

Future Potential for Patient Care Enhancements

The future of healthcare is set for major changes driven by AI innovations. Several promising areas include:

- **Remote Monitoring**: Wearable devices equipped with AI capabilities continuously monitor vital signs and alert healthcare providers to potential issues before they become critical. This is particularly beneficial for managing chronic conditions such as diabetes or hypertension.

- **Virtual Health Assistants**: Chatbots powered by Natural Language Processing (NLP) assist patients in managing their health by providing real-time information and support. These virtual assistants can schedule appointments, remind patients to take medications, and answer health-related queries.

- **Predictive Analytics**: By analyzing historical patient data,

AI models predict disease outbreaks or hospital admission rates. This proactive approach helps healthcare systems allocate resources efficiently and prepare for surges in demand.

Investments in these technologies promise not only improved patient outcomes but also enhanced operational efficiency within healthcare systems.

Real World Examples

Several notable implementations of AI in healthcare underscore its transformative potential:

- **Google DeepMind's AlphaFold** accurately predicts protein folding structures, accelerating biomedical research.

- **Arterys** utilizes cloud-based deep learning algorithms to analyze medical imaging data across multiple modalities in near real-time.

- **PathAI** enhances the diagnostic accuracy of pathologists through machine learning models that identify disease markers in tissue samples.

As these examples illustrate, the integration of AI into healthcare practices heralds a new era of precision medicine and patient-centric care.

The implications are profound—not just for diagnostics but across all facets of patient care—from personalized treatment regimens to predictive analytics that foresee medical complications before they arise. This paradigm shift underscores the importance of continued investment in AI research within the healthcare sector.

AI in Finance: Trading, Risk Management, and Fraud Detection

The integration of **finance technology** has transformed the financial sector, with **algorithmic trading** and **fraud prevention** being key areas of application. The combination of AI and finance showcases both the immense possibilities and the pressing challenges faced by the industry.

Use of AI in Trading Strategies and Risk Assessment

Algorithmic trading uses AI to execute trades at speeds and frequencies that are unrealistic for human traders. By examining large amounts of data to find patterns and trends, AI-powered systems can make instant decisions that improve trading strategies.

Key Applications:

- **High-frequency trading (HFT)**: Uses algorithms to trade large volumes of stocks in milliseconds. Firms using HFT gain an advantage by taking advantage of tiny price differences.

- **Predictive analytics**: AI models forecast market movements based on past data, current market conditions, and even social media sentiment. This foresight allows traders to position themselves favorably.

- **Risk management algorithms**: These evaluate potential

risks associated with trades by analyzing market volatility, credit risk, and other financial indicators. This capability ensures more informed decision-making.

Impact on Financial Decision-Making Processes

AI's influence goes beyond automated trading; it fundamentally changes how decisions are made within financial institutions. Traditional methods often relied heavily on human intuition and manual analysis. AI introduces a data-driven approach that enhances precision and efficiency.

Areas of Transformation:

- **Portfolio management**: Robo-advisors customize investment portfolios based on an individual's risk tolerance, financial goals, and market conditions. They continuously adjust portfolios to maintain optimal performance.

- **Credit scoring**: Machine learning algorithms assess creditworthiness by analyzing non-traditional data sources such as social media activity or utility payments, providing a more comprehensive risk profile.

- **Sentiment analysis**: AI tools evaluate public sentiment regarding financial markets through natural language processing (NLP) techniques applied to news articles, forums, and social media posts. This insight informs strategic decisions.

Case Studies on Successful Implementations

Several real-world examples highlight the effectiveness of AI in finance:

1. **JPMorgan Chase's COiN Platform:**

- JPMorgan Chase developed the Contract Intelligence (COiN) platform to analyze legal documents and extract critical data points. This task previously required 360,000 hours of work annually from lawyers and loan officers.

- The implementation of COiN not only reduced labor costs but also minimized errors associated with manual document review.

1. **BlackRock's Aladdin System:**

- BlackRock utilizes its Aladdin platform for portfolio management, risk assessment, and trading operations. Aladdin processes millions of trades daily and manages over $21 trillion in assets.

- The system integrates data analytics with machine learning to provide real-time insights into asset performance, ensuring optimal investment strategies.

1. **PayPal's Fraud Detection Algorithms:**

- PayPal employs sophisticated machine learning algorithms to detect fraudulent transactions in real-time. These algorithms analyze transaction patterns, user behavior, and geographical data points.

- Since adopting AI-driven fraud detection measures, PayPal

has significantly reduced fraudulent activities while maintaining a smooth user experience for legitimate transactions.

AI continues to reshape the finance landscape by providing tools that enhance accuracy, efficiency, and security. As these technologies evolve, their role in algorithmic trading, risk management, and fraud prevention will become even more pivotal.

Ethical Considerations in AI: Privacy, Bias, and Decision-Making

Artificial intelligence has the power to bring about significant change, but it also presents serious **ethical challenges**. These challenges can be grouped into three main areas: privacy issues, algorithmic bias, and decision-making transparency.

Privacy Issues

AI systems often rely on large amounts of data to function effectively. This reliance raises important *privacy concerns*:

- **Data Collection:** AI technologies such as facial recognition and social media algorithms collect extensive personal data. The question arises: who owns this data?

- **Data Usage:** Even if consent is obtained for data collection, how that data is used can still infringe on individual privacy. For instance, targeted advertising based on browsing history can feel invasive.

- **Security Risks:** Collected data is susceptible to breaches, leading to potential misuse or theft of sensitive information.

Edward Snowden, a notable whistleblower, once remarked:

"When you collect everything, you understand nothing."

This highlights the paradox of big data—greater collection does not always equate to greater insight.

Algorithmic Bias

The issue of *algorithmic bias* is another pressing concern. Since AI systems learn from existing data, they can inadvertently perpetuate historical biases:

- **Training Data:** If the training dataset is biased, the AI will likely replicate those biases. For example, facial recognition systems have been shown to misidentify people of color at higher rates.

- **Decision-Making:** Biased algorithms can lead to unfair outcomes in crucial areas like hiring processes, loan approvals, and criminal sentencing.

A vivid case illustrating this was when Amazon's recruitment algorithm was found to discriminate against female candidates because it had been trained primarily on resumes submitted by men over a ten-year period. This incident underscores the importance of scrutinizing the datasets used in AI training.

Decision-Making Transparency

Transparency and accountability are vital for ethical AI deployment:

- **Opaque Algorithms:** Many AI systems operate as "black boxes," making it difficult to understand how decisions are made. This lack of transparency can erode trust.

- **Accountability:** When an AI system makes a mistake—such as misdiagnosing a patient or erroneously denying a loan—determining who is accountable becomes complex.

To build trust and ensure fairness, organizations must adopt practices that promote transparency. This involves clearly explaining how algorithms function and being open about their limitations.

Real-Life Examples Highlighting Ethical Failures

Several high-profile incidents have shed light on these ethical challenges:

1. **Cambridge Analytica Scandal:** Personal data from millions of Facebook users was harvested without consent to influence political campaigns. This breach highlighted severe privacy concerns.

2. **COMPAS Recidivism Algorithm:** Used in US courts to predict the likelihood of re-offending, this tool was found to be biased against African American defendants.

3. **Google Photos Tagging Incident:** Google's image-recognition algorithm mistakenly tagged photos of black individuals as gorillas, sparking outrage and highlighting the dire consequences of biased training data.

These examples underscore that ethical failures in AI are not just hypothetical scenarios but real-world issues with profound implications.

Importance of Transparency & Accountability

Ensuring ethical use of AI requires concerted effort across multiple fronts:

- **Regulatory Oversight:** Governments and regulatory bodies must establish guidelines that mandate transparency and accountability.

- **Ethical Frameworks:** Organizations should develop robust ethical frameworks for AI development and deployment.

- **Public Awareness:** Educating the public about the potential risks and benefits of AI fosters informed decision-making and societal trust.

In addressing these ethical dilemmas, we must remember that technology itself is neutral; its impact depends on how it is used. As we navigate this complex landscape, prioritizing ethical considerations will help us harness AI's potential while mitigating its risks effectively.

Economic Impact of AI: Job Displacement and Creation

Artificial Intelligence (AI) is changing the economy in significant ways, especially when it comes to jobs. Automation, which is a big part of AI, is changing industries by making processes more efficient and reducing the need for humans in repetitive tasks. This change has led to discussions about job loss in various fields.

Automation and Job Displacement

AI-driven automation affects different sectors in different ways:

- **Manufacturing**: Robots and AI systems are taking over assembly lines, leading to significant reductions in manual labor.

- **Retail**: Self-checkout systems and inventory management algorithms reduce the necessity for cashier roles.

- **Customer Service**: Chatbots and virtual assistants handle routine inquiries, diminishing the demand for call center employees.

While these advancements improve efficiency, they also displace workers who once performed these tasks. According to a report by the World Economic Forum, up to 85 million jobs could be displaced by 2025 due to technological changes.

New Jobs Created Through Technological Advancements

Despite concerns about job displacement, AI also generates new employment opportunities. The digital transformation creates roles that require a blend of technical skills and human creativity:

- **Data Scientists**: Professionals who analyze complex datasets to derive actionable insights.

- **AI Specialists**: Experts developing and maintaining AI algorithms and models.

- **Cybersecurity Analysts**: Guardians against cyber threats heightened by increased digital reliance.

These emerging roles underscore a dynamic job market where technology both eliminates and creates employment opportunities. A study by Gartner predicts that AI will create more jobs than it eliminates by 2022, signaling a net positive effect on employment.

Skills Needed to Thrive Amidst Changes

As AI continues to evolve, the skills required to thrive in this landscape shift accordingly. Several competencies become indispensable:

1. **Technical Proficiency**:

- *Programming Languages*: Python, R, and Java are essential for developing AI models.

- *Machine Learning*: Understanding algorithms and data processing is crucial.

1. **Analytical Thinking**:

- *Problem-Solving*: Ability to approach complex issues logically.

- *Data Analysis*: Interpreting large volumes of data effectively.

1. **Soft Skills**:

- *Adaptability*: Willingness to learn and adapt to new technologies.

- *Creativity*: Innovating solutions where AI falls short.

By investing in education and continuous learning, individuals can better prepare for an AI-driven economy. Companies like Google offer online courses through platforms like Coursera, emphasizing the importance of lifelong learning in adapting to technological changes.

Balancing Job Market Transformation

The duality of job displacement and creation necessitates a balanced approach from policymakers and industry leaders. Initiatives such as reskilling programs can mitigate the adverse effects on displaced workers while capitalizing on new employment avenues created by AI advancements.

A notable example is Amazon's $700 million investment in retraining one-third of its U.S. workforce by 2025. This program aims to equip employees with skills for higher-paying tech roles within the company or elsewhere.

Navigating the economic impact of AI requires a nuanced understanding of both its disruptive potential and innovative promise. By anticipating these shifts, societies can harness AI's benefits while mitigating its challenges, ensuring an inclusive transition into this technologically advanced era.

Social Implications of AI: Changes in Daily Life

Artificial Intelligence (AI) is not just a technological marvel; it is a transformative force altering the fabric of our daily lives. The integration of AI into various aspects of society yields profound shifts in how we interact, make decisions, and perceive the world around us.

Alteration of Daily Interactions

AI has seamlessly woven itself into the tapestry of our everyday routines. Consider virtual assistants like Siri, Alexa, and Google Assistant. These digital entities streamline tasks from setting reminders to controlling smart home devices. **Voice-activated commands** have become second nature, reducing the need for physical interaction with technology.

- **Smartphones** equipped with AI features suggest personalized content, optimize battery usage, and even predict user needs.

- **Social media platforms** utilize AI algorithms to curate feeds, recommend friends, and filter content based on user behavior.

- **Navigation apps** powered by AI offer real-time traffic updates and alternative routes, enhancing commuting efficiency.

These innovations reflect a broader trend: human behavior adapting to an increasingly automated environment. The convenience brought by AI fosters dependency but also raises questions about our diminishing role in routine decision-making processes.

Effects on Social Structures & Relationships

The ripple effect of AI's prevalence extends to social structures and relationships. Communication patterns evolve as people engage more with digital interfaces than face-to-face interactions. **Chatbots** and automated customer service agents replace human interaction in commercial settings, affecting employment landscapes and customer experiences.

- **Online dating platforms** harness AI to match individuals based on compatibility algorithms, transforming romantic pursuits.

- **Social networks** employ machine learning to detect harmful content, promoting safer online environments but also sparking debates about free speech.

- **Virtual reality (VR) and augmented reality (AR)** applications create immersive experiences that redefine entertainment and social engagement.

This shift towards digital communication can lead to a sense of isolation despite being hyper-connected online. Traditional social bonds may weaken as virtual interactions become more prevalent, challenging the essence of human connection.

Predictions About Long-term Societal Transformations

The long-term societal transformations driven by AI promise both opportunities and challenges. As AI systems become more sophisticated, they will likely influence various sectors beyond current expectations.

1. **Education:** Personalized learning experiences through AI

tutors could revolutionize education but necessitate new pedagogical approaches.

2. **Healthcare:** Predictive analytics might enhance preventive care yet require robust ethical guidelines to manage sensitive health data.

3. **Workplace:** Autonomous systems could lead to decentralized work environments, demanding adaptability from the workforce.

These predictions underscore the dual-edged nature of AI's impact—enhancing efficiency while posing ethical dilemmas. As we navigate these changes, society must balance technological advancements with human values to ensure equitable progress.

Understanding the social implications of AI is crucial for grasping its full potential and addressing its challenges. By examining how daily interactions are altered, observing effects on social structures and relationships, and predicting long-term transformations, we gain a comprehensive view of this dynamic landscape.

"Technology is best when it brings people together."

— Matt Mullenweg

As we stand at this crossroads, harnessing AI's capabilities responsibly will shape a future where technology serves humanity without compromising our core values.

Jobs That Will Be Replaced by AI

Data Entry and Clerical Work

D ata entry is a fundamental part of clerical jobs. It involves the careful process of entering, updating, and managing data within systems. These roles require both accuracy and speed to ensure important information is recorded correctly and easily accessible. Common tasks include:

- Entering data from paper documents into digital systems

- Updating records in databases

- Transcribing information from audio recordings

- Managing spreadsheets and databases

- Processing invoices and other financial documents

Because these tasks are repetitive, they are ideal candidates for automation.

Automation Potential in Clerical Roles

AI automation has the potential to transform clerical work by improving efficiency and reducing human error. The structured and repetitive nature of data entry tasks makes them highly suitable for automation. Here are some key benefits:

- **Increased Speed:** AI can process large amounts of data much faster than humans.

- **Enhanced Accuracy:** Automated systems reduce errors caused by manual data entry.

- **Cost Savings:** Less reliance on extensive human labor leads to lower operational costs.

This shift could significantly change the roles of clerical workers, moving them towards more strategic responsibilities.

Examples of AI Tools That Streamline Data Entry Processes

Several AI tools have emerged as leaders in automating data entry processes. These tools use machine learning and natural language processing to achieve high levels of accuracy and efficiency. Some notable examples include:

1. **UiPath:**

- Specializes in robotic process automation (RPA).

- Automates various repetitive tasks including data extraction from PDFs and structured documents.

- Known for its user-friendly interface that allows non-programmers to create automated workflows.

1. **ABBYY FlexiCapture:**

- Utilizes advanced optical character recognition (OCR) technology.

- Capable of extracting data from complex documents with high precision.

- Supports a wide range of formats including handwritten text.

1. **Blue Prism:**

- Another prominent RPA tool.

- Focuses on large-scale enterprise solutions.

- Integrates seamlessly with existing IT infrastructure to automate end-to-end processes.

1. **HyperScience:**

- Employs machine learning algorithms to convert handwritten and printed documents into digital text.

- Known for its high accuracy rates even with challenging document types.

These tools not only make data entry more efficient but also free up clerical staff to engage in higher-value activities, such as data analysis and strategic planning.

Real-World Examples

Here are two real-world examples illustrating the impact of AI tools on clerical work:

1. A global logistics company used **UiPath** to automate invoice processing, resulting in a 70% reduction in processing time and fewer errors.

2. A healthcare provider implemented **ABBYY FlexiCapture** to digitize patient records, enabling quicker access to medical histories and better patient care.

Future Implications

As AI continues to develop, its role in clerical work will expand beyond just data entry. Future advancements may see AI taking on more complex tasks such as scheduling meetings, managing communications, and making preliminary decisions based on analyzed data trends.

For professionals in these roles, adapting to this shift means acquiring new skills in overseeing AI systems and strategic management—ensuring they remain valuable members of an increasingly automated workplace.

The changes brought about by AI in the field of data entry demonstrate how technology reshapes job markets. It highlights the importance of continuous learning and adaptability amidst rapid technological changes.

Customer Service and Support

Impact of AI on Customer Service Roles

The introduction of **AI in customer service** has significantly transformed the landscape of support roles. Traditional customer service often involves answering repetitive questions, handling complaints, and processing requests. These tasks are increasingly being automated, leading to job displacement for many workers.

AI-driven chatbots and virtual assistants are capable of handling these interactions with a high degree of accuracy and efficiency. For instance, AI can process natural language to understand customer queries and provide instant responses, reducing the need for human intervention. This not only speeds up response times but also allows human agents to focus on more complex issues.

Key Points

- **Efficiency**: AI can handle thousands of inquiries simultaneously, something impossible for human agents.

- **Consistency**: Chatbots provide uniform responses, ensuring that customers receive consistent information.

- **Scalability**: AI systems can easily scale to meet increasing demand without the need for additional hiring.

Evolution of Support Systems Through AI

Support systems have evolved from simple automated phone menus to sophisticated AI-driven platforms. Modern AI tools integrate machine learning algorithms that continuously improve based on customer interactions. This evolution signifies a shift from reactive to proactive support systems.

Proactive support involves anticipating customer needs before they arise. For example, AI can analyze user behavior to detect potential issues and offer solutions preemptively. This predictive capability enhances the customer experience by minimizing disruptions and providing timely assistance.

Case Studies of Successful AI Implementations in Customer Service

Successful implementation of AI in customer service can be observed across various industries:

1. **Banking Sector:**

- *Bank of America*: The bank's virtual assistant, Erica, uses AI to help customers with transactions, bill payments, and financial advice. Erica successfully handled over 50 million client requests within its first year.

1. **E-commerce Industry:**

- *Amazon*: The e-commerce giant uses AI-powered chatbots to manage a myriad of customer service tasks, from tracking orders to resolving issues with purchases. These bots handle millions of queries daily, significantly reducing the workload on human agents.

1. **Telecommunications:**

- *Vodafone*: The telecom company implemented an AI chat-

bot named TOBi which assists customers with troubleshooting network problems and managing account details. TOBi was able to resolve up to 70% of inquiries without
human intervention in its initial rollout phase.

Real-World Examples Highlighting Efficiency and Scalability

Example 1: A multinational telecommunications company reported
a 30% reduction in call center volume after deploying an AI-driven
chatbot capable of resolving common customer issues autonomously.

Example 2: An online retailer saw a 20% increase in customer satisfaction scores following the implementation of an AI system designed
to provide instant answers about product availability and shipping
details.

These case studies underscore the transformative potential of AI in
enhancing operational efficiency while scaling services effectively.

Future Prospects

The continuous advancement of AI technology promises even greater
integration into the realm of customer service. As machine learning
models become more sophisticated, we can expect further improvements in how support is delivered:

- **Personalization**: Enhanced algorithms will allow for highly
  personalized interactions based on individual customer data.

- **Multilingual Support**: Advanced language processing capabilities will enable seamless support across different lan-

guages.

- **Emotional Intelligence**: Future iterations may include components that gauge sentiment and tone, allowing for more empathetic interactions.

The rise of **AI in customer service** marks a pivotal shift towards more efficient and scalable support systems. While this evolution brings about significant benefits in terms of speed and consistency, it also poses challenges related to job displacement that must be addressed thoughtfully as technology continues to advance.

Basic Manufacturing and Assembly Line Jobs

Overview of Manufacturing Tasks Prone to Automation

Manufacturing jobs often involve repetitive tasks that follow a predictable pattern. These roles are prime candidates for automation due to the structured nature of their processes. Typical tasks include:

- **Assembly Line Operations**: Workers assemble parts to create finished products.

- **Quality Control Inspections**: Ensuring that products meet specified standards.

- **Packaging and Sorting**: Organizing products for shipping or further processing.

These tasks require precision and consistency, attributes that machines can replicate with high efficiency.

The Role of Robotics in Replacing Manual Labor

Robotics plays a pivotal role in transforming manufacturing environments. Robots bring numerous advantages:

- **Accuracy and Speed**: Machines operate with a level of precision unattainable by human hands, reducing errors and increasing production speed.

- **Cost Efficiency**: While the initial investment in robotics can be substantial, the long-term savings from reduced labor costs and increased productivity are significant.

- **24/7 Operations**: Unlike human workers, robots do not require breaks, enabling continuous production cycles.

For instance, automotive manufacturers like Tesla use robots extensively for tasks ranging from welding car frames to installing windshields. This integration leads to more efficient production lines and higher-quality outputs.

Future Trends in Automated Manufacturing

The horizon of automated manufacturing is ever-expanding, driven by advancements in technology. Key trends include:

1. **Collaborative Robots (Cobots)**: Unlike traditional industrial robots that operate in isolation, cobots work alongside human workers. They assist with strenuous tasks, enhancing both safety and productivity.

2. **Artificial Intelligence Integration**: AI systems analyze

data from manufacturing processes to optimize performance. Predictive maintenance powered by AI can foresee equipment failures before they occur, minimizing downtime.

3. **Advanced Sensor Technology**: Sensors embedded in machinery provide real-time data on performance metrics. This information ensures that every aspect of the production process is monitored and optimized continuously.

Notably, companies like Siemens are at the forefront of these innovations. Their "Digital Factory" concept incorporates AI, IoT (Internet of Things), and advanced robotics to create a seamless manufacturing ecosystem.

By embracing these trends, manufacturers can achieve unprecedented levels of efficiency and adaptability in their operations.

The transition from manual labor to automated systems in manufacturing is not merely a shift but a revolution that redefines the industry landscape. The future promises even greater integration of cutting-edge technologies that will continue to shape how we produce goods on a global scale.

Retail Sales and Cashier Positions

Retail jobs, especially cashier positions, are at the forefront of change driven by AI. New AI technologies are reshaping how transactions happen, affecting the roles that human staff traditionally held.

Changes in Retail Due to AI-Driven Checkouts

AI-driven checkouts are transforming retail by making the purchasing process more efficient. Self-checkout systems powered by advanced machine learning algorithms can identify products, calculate prices, and complete transactions without needing a human operator. A prime example of this shift is seen in Amazon Go stores, which use sensors and computer vision technology to create a smooth "just walk out" shopping experience. Customers no longer have to stand in line or interact with cashiers, as AI takes care of every part of the checkout process.

Key Benefits:

- *Efficiency*: Faster checkout times reduce customer wait times.

- *Accuracy*: Minimizes human error in transaction processing.

- *Cost Savings*: Reduces the need for multiple cashier positions.

The Role of Virtual Assistants in Enhancing Customer Experience

Virtual assistants play a crucial role in improving customer experience within retail settings. These AI-powered tools help customers with questions, recommend products, and even provide personalized shopping advice. Chatbots on e-commerce websites guide users through selecting products and completing purchases, while digital kiosks in stores offer immediate assistance and information.

Impactful Applications:

- *24/7 Availability*: Virtual assistants offer continuous support without breaks.

- *Personalization*: Tailor recommendations based on customer preferences and purchase history.

- *Consistency*: Deliver uniform service quality across all interactions.

Job Implications for Cashiers and Retail Staff

The introduction of AI technologies into retail operations has significant consequences for traditional roles like cashiers and sales associates. While some jobs may become unnecessary due to automation, new opportunities emerge in areas that require human understanding and complex problem-solving abilities.

Potential Outcomes:

1. **Job Displacement:**

- Cashier roles face a high risk of reduction as self-checkout systems become common.

- Routine tasks like scanning items and handling payments are automated.

1. **Role Evolution:**

- Retail staff may transition to roles focused on customer engagement and support.

- Employees can take on responsibilities involving merchandising, store management, and personalized customer service.

1. **Skill Development:**

- Training programs focusing on digital literacy and technical skills prepare employees for new roles.

- Emphasis on soft skills like communication and problem-solving enhances workforce adaptability.

Real-World Examples

Many retailers have successfully implemented AI solutions to improve efficiency:

1. **Walmart**:

- Uses shelf-scanning robots to monitor inventory levels and restock items efficiently.

- Employs autonomous floor cleaners to maintain store hygiene without human supervision.

1. **Sephora**:

- Introduced virtual try-on features powered by augmented reality (AR) to allow customers to visualize products before purchase.

- Uses AI-driven chatbots for personalized beauty advice and product recommendations.

Future Outlook

The impact of AI on retail jobs is constantly evolving, presenting both challenges and opportunities. While automation may decrease certain positions, it also encourages innovation in customer service roles that utilize human creativity and emotional intelligence.

Examining how these trends develop in other industries reveals wider implications for job markets across various sectors.

Routine Administrative Tasks

Automation is changing the way we handle routine **administrative tasks**, making offices more efficient and changing job roles in companies. The ability of AI to make boring tasks easier could completely change how administrative work is done.

Common Administrative Tasks Susceptible to AI Replacement

Administrative jobs often include repetitive, time-consuming tasks that are perfect for automation. These tasks include:

- **Data Entry**: Manually inputting data into systems is both monotonous and prone to error. AI can automate this process, ensuring accuracy and saving time.

- **Scheduling**: Coordinating meetings and managing calendars can be labor-intensive. AI-powered tools like *Calendly* or *Google Assistant* simplify this by automating scheduling based on availability and preferences.

- **Email Management**: Sorting through emails, categorizing them, and responding to routine inquiries are tasks that AI can handle efficiently. Tools like *SaneBox* and *Boomerang* categorize emails and automate responses.

- **Document Management**: Organizing, retrieving, and updating documents can be streamlined using AI-driven document management systems such as *M-Files* or *DocuWare*.

Tools That Automate Scheduling and Communications

Several AI tools have emerged to enhance office efficiency by automating scheduling and communications. These tools not only save time
but also improve accuracy and consistency in administrative processes:

1. **AI Schedulers**:

- *X.AI*: An AI personal assistant that schedules meetings by
coordinating with all parties involved via email.

- *Clara*: Utilizes natural language processing (NLP) to schedule meetings seamlessly.

1. **Communication Automation**:

- *Slack Bots*: Automate reminders, notifications, and follow-ups within the Slack communication platform.

- *Chatbots*: Deployed on websites or internal systems to handle
routine queries, freeing up human resources for more complex issues.

1. **Virtual Assistants**:

- *Google Assistant* and *Amazon Alexa*: Assist in managing
tasks such as setting reminders, sending messages, and re-

trieving information.

The Future of Administrative Roles in a Tech-Driven Workplace

The integration of AI into administrative tasks raises questions about the future landscape of these roles. While automation will undoubtedly reduce the need for manual intervention in routine tasks, it will also create opportunities for administrative professionals to engage in more strategic functions:

- **Shift Towards Strategic Roles**: As routine tasks are automated, administrative professionals can focus on higher-value activities such as project management, process improvement, and strategic planning.

- **Skill Enhancement**: The demand for skills in managing AI tools and interpreting their outputs will grow. Training programs will be essential to equip administrative staff with these new competencies.

- **Hybrid Work Models**: A blend of human oversight with automated processes will likely become the norm. Humans will provide the critical thinking and emotional intelligence that machines lack.

Real-World Examples

Organizations across various industries have begun adopting AI tools to automate routine administrative tasks:

- **IBM Watson**: Utilized by IBM for internal operations to automate HR processes such as employee onboarding and training.

- **Salesforce Einstein**: Implemented within Salesforce CRM to automate customer relationship management tasks like lead scoring and email follow-ups.

Implications for Office Efficiency

AI's role in automating routine administrative work extends beyond mere efficiency gains:

- **Cost Reduction**: Reduced need for manual labor translates into lower operational costs.

- **Enhanced Accuracy**: Minimization of human error results in more reliable data handling.

- **Employee Satisfaction**: By offloading mundane tasks, employees can engage in more fulfilling work.

As organizations continue to integrate AI into their workflows, the transformation of routine administrative tasks will exemplify the broader shift towards a tech-driven workplace where efficiency meets innovation.

Basic Financial Analysis and Accounting

How AI Performs Basic Financial Analysis More Efficiently

AI has transformed the world of financial analysis. Instead of manually going through spreadsheets and interpreting data, we now have advanced algorithms that can quickly process large amounts of information. These machine learning models can spot patterns and trends that human analysts might miss, offering insights with unmatched accuracy. This efficiency is not just about being fast; it's also about being precise. AI's ability to analyze past data and forecast future market trends reduces the chances of mistakes, making financial analysis more trustworthy.

Tools That Assist Accountants with Routine Tasks

Using AI in accounting isn't just something for the future; it's happening right now with several tools already changing the industry:

- **QuickBooks Online**: Uses machine learning to automate tasks like categorizing expenses and matching transactions, allowing accountants to concentrate on more strategic work.

- **Xero**: Employs AI to make bank reconciliation processes smoother, significantly cutting down on time spent on manual checks.

- **KPMG's Clara**: An intelligent audit platform that uses AI to analyze large datasets, ensuring compliance and identifying potential risks.

These tools show how AI is getting rid of repetitive tasks, letting accountants use their skills for more complex problem-solving.

Implications for the Accounting Profession Moving Forward

The integration of AI into financial analysis and accounting marks a significant shift in the profession. While some may fear job displacement, the reality points towards an evolution rather than extinction. Accountants are transitioning from number-crunchers to strategic advisors. The role now demands a higher level of analytical thinking and business insight.

Strategic Implications:

- **Enhanced Decision-Making**: With AI handling routine tasks, accountants can provide more in-depth financial advice, influencing key business decisions.

- **Skill Development**: The demand for skills such as data analysis, critical thinking, and expertise in AI tools is surging.

- **Job Reallocation**: Instead of eliminating jobs, AI is reallocating them towards more value-added activities like financial planning and advisory services.

The profession is witnessing a paradigm shift. Accountants who embrace these changes and adapt by enhancing their skill sets will find themselves at the forefront of this transformation.

Integrating AI into financial analysis and accounting not only augments efficiency but also redefines professional roles within the industry. It's a testament to how technology can elevate human potential when leveraged appropriately.

Transportation and Delivery Services

Overview of Transportation Roles at Risk from Automation

Transportation jobs have long been a cornerstone of the global economy, employing millions in roles ranging from truck drivers to delivery personnel. These positions involve repetitive tasks such as driving, route planning, and package handling—making them highly susceptible to automation. AI-driven technologies and autonomous vehicles are rapidly transforming this landscape.

Key transportation roles at risk include:

- **Truck drivers**: Long-haul trucking is a prime candidate for automation due to its repetitive nature and the pressing need for efficiency.

- **Delivery drivers**: Local delivery services can benefit significantly from autonomous vehicles and drones.

- **Taxi and rideshare drivers**: Autonomous taxis are disrupting traditional ride-hailing services.

The Rise of Autonomous Delivery Systems

The development of autonomous delivery systems is reshaping how goods are transported. Self-driving trucks, delivery drones, and robots are no longer concepts confined to science fiction but active components in logistics chains.

Notable advancements include:

- **Self-driving trucks**: Companies like *Waymo* and *TuSimple* are pioneering self-driving trucks that promise to enhance efficiency while reducing human error.

- **Delivery drones**: *Amazon Prime Air* aims to revolutionize last-mile delivery with drones capable of delivering packages within 30 minutes.

- **Autonomous robots**: *Starship Technologies* has deployed delivery robots on college campuses and urban areas, offering a glimpse into the future of local deliveries.

Case Studies on Companies Implementing These Technologies

Several companies have already begun integrating AI into their transportation and delivery processes, setting benchmarks for the industry.

Waymo

Waymo, a subsidiary of Alphabet Inc., has been testing its autonomous trucks across various states in the U.S. Their self-driving technology boasts millions of miles driven autonomously, combining machine learning algorithms with real-time data processing to navigate complex road conditions.

> "Our mission is to make it safe and easy for people and things to move around," says Waymo CEO John Krafcik. "Autonomous trucks can revolutionize logistics by reducing costs and increasing reliability."

Amazon Prime Air

Amazon's drone program represents a significant leap forward in last-mile delivery. These drones use advanced AI for navigation, obstacle avoidance, and efficient route planning. While regulatory hurdles remain, Amazon continues to push the envelope on what's possible with autonomous aerial deliveries.

Starship Technologies

Starship Technologies' ground-based delivery robots exemplify practical applications of AI in local deliveries. These robots navigate sidewalks using computer vision and GPS, delivering food and parcels within short distances. The success on college campuses indicates scalability potential for broader urban use.

Simple Legal Research and Document Review

Legal research is a fundamental part of being a lawyer. It often requires going through large databases, case files, and legal documents to find relevant information. This job has traditionally been done by paralegals and junior lawyers, but now more and more of it is being done by machines. With the rise of AI in legal research, it's become much easier and faster to find important legal cases and laws.

How AI is Making Legal Research Faster

AI tools use technology to read and understand legal documents faster and more accurately than people can. These tools can analyze huge

amounts of data at speeds that humans can't match. Here are some
ways AI is improving legal research:

- **Predicting Case Outcomes**: AI can look at past cases and
  predict how similar cases might turn out, giving lawyers useful information for their arguments.

- **Finding Patterns in Decisions**: Machine learning algorithms can spot trends in court decisions that human re-
  searchers might overlook.

One example of this is *ROSS Intelligence*, an AI-powered legal research tool that uses IBM's Watson to understand questions asked in
plain language. ROSS then searches through millions of documents
to provide exact answers, greatly reducing the time spent on research.

Tools Making Document Review Easier

Document review is another area in law that can benefit from automation. Going through contracts, discovery documents, and other
legal papers can take a lot of time and be prone to mistakes. AI tools
are changing this process by:

- **Using E-discovery Software**: Programs like *Relativi-
  ty* and *Everlaw* use AI to find relevant documents from large
  sets of data.

- **Analyzing Contracts Automatically**: Solutions like *Kira
  Systems* automatically pull out important sections from
  contracts for quicker review.

These tools use advanced technology to scan documents for specific words or irregularities. This not only speeds up the document review process but also improves accuracy by reducing human error.

The Future for Paralegals and Legal Assistants

The growth of AI in legal research and document review doesn't mean that paralegals or legal assistants will lose their jobs. Instead, it will change what they do. While some basic tasks may disappear, new opportunities will arise:

1. **More Complex Work**: With AI taking care of simple tasks, paralegals can focus on more complicated duties like talking to clients and planning strategies.

2. **Need for Tech-Savvy Workers**: There will be a greater need for paralegals who know how to use AI tools, which means ongoing training will be necessary.

Law schools are already changing their programs to teach students about these new technologies. For example, the University of Southern California's Gould School of Law offers classes specifically aimed at teaching students how AI is used in law.

Real-Life Examples

Law firms such as *Baker McKenzie* have successfully integrated AI into their operations. They use RAVN, an AI platform, to streamline document review processes, enabling them to manage larger workloads more efficiently.

The introduction of AI into legal research and document review marks a significant change within the industry. By improving speed and precision, these technologies allow lawyers to offer better services while adapting to an ever-changing environment.

This smooth transition from transportation automation to advancements in law shows how widely spread the influence of AI is across different industries.

Radiology and Basic Medical Diagnostics

Role of AI in Medical Imaging Interpretation

Radiology jobs are experiencing a paradigm shift due to advancements in artificial intelligence. AI algorithms have proven highly effective in interpreting medical images, ranging from X-rays to MRIs. These systems can analyze vast amounts of data at unprecedented speeds, identifying patterns and anomalies that might be missed by the human eye. For instance, Google's DeepMind has developed an AI that can detect over 50 different eye diseases from optical coherence tomography scans with remarkable accuracy.

Benefits of Automating Diagnostic Processes

Automating diagnostic processes offers several benefits, not least of which is increasing efficiency. Traditional radiology tasks often involve time-consuming image analysis, a process that can significantly delay patient care. AI-driven diagnostic tools can expedite this process, providing real-time results and enabling quicker medical interventions.

Some tangible benefits include:

- **Higher Accuracy**: AI systems reduce the risk of human error, offering more reliable diagnoses.

- **Cost Efficiency**: Minimizing the need for repeated tests lowers healthcare costs.

- **Scalability**: AI tools can easily be scaled across various healthcare settings, from small clinics to large hospitals.

A study published in *The Lancet Digital Health* revealed that AI models outperformed radiologists in diagnosing certain conditions like pneumonia from chest X-rays. This suggests a future where AI could complement or even replace some aspects of radiological diagnostics.

Future Implications for Radiologists in Healthcare Settings

The rise of medical diagnostics AI impacts the role of radiologists in complex ways. While some fear job displacement, the reality is often more nuanced. Instead of rendering radiologists obsolete, AI is likely to serve as an invaluable tool that enhances their capabilities.

Key future implications include:

- **Enhanced Decision-Making**: Radiologists can focus on more complex cases requiring nuanced judgment while relying on AI for routine tasks.

- **Continuous Learning**: As AI systems evolve, so too will the skill sets required by radiologists, necessitating ongoing education.

- **Collaborative Workflows**: Future healthcare settings may see a seamless integration of human expertise and machine precision, leading to more collaborative workflows.

Dr. Eric Topol, a renowned cardiologist and author of *Deep Medicine*, argues that "AI will make healthcare more human" by freeing up physicians to spend more time on patient interaction rather than administrative tasks.

The future landscape of radiology jobs may thus be characterized by a symbiotic relationship between human professionals and advanced technologies. Embracing this evolution requires an open mind and a willingness to adapt—a challenge but also an opportunity to redefine what it means to be a healthcare provider in the 21st century.

Telemarketing and Sales Calls

How Telemarketing is Evolving with AI Solutions

Telemarketing, traditionally associated with persistent calls and scripted pitches, is undergoing a radical transformation. AI-driven solutions are stepping into roles once dominated by human agents, bringing efficiency and consistency to the forefront.

AI Chatbots and **voice assistants** now handle initial customer interactions, leveraging natural language processing (NLP) to understand and respond to queries. These AI systems can manage thousands of calls simultaneously, ensuring no potential lead is left untapped. Unlike human agents, these systems never tire or deviate from the script, providing a uniform experience.

Effectiveness of AI-Driven Sales Calls Compared to Human Agents

AI's role in sales calls extends beyond mere automation. Its effectiveness can be dissected into several layers:

1. **Data Analytics**: AI systems analyze vast amounts of data to identify patterns and predict which leads are most likely to convert. This predictive capability allows for targeted, high-impact interactions.

2. **Customization**: Despite being automated, AI-driven calls can offer a personalized experience. By utilizing customer data, these systems tailor conversations to resonate with individual preferences and past behaviors.

3. **Consistency**: AI ensures that every call adheres to best practices without deviation, leading to higher success rates in lead conversion.

While human agents bring empathy and adaptability to the table, AI boasts an edge in speed, accuracy, and scalability. A hybrid model where AI handles preliminary interactions followed by human engagement for complex queries could harness the strengths of both.

Long-Term Outlook for Telemarketers

The rise of AI in telemarketing prompts significant questions about the future landscape of this field:

1. **Job Displacement vs. Job Evolution**: As routine tasks become automated, telemarketers may find their roles evolving rather than disappearing. Focus might shift towards managing AI systems, interpreting data analytics results, or handling complex customer interactions that require a human touch.

2. **Skill Development**: The necessity for telemarketers to upskill becomes evident. Understanding how to work alongside AI tools will be crucial. Training programs focused on
digital literacy and advanced communication skills will likely
emerge as essential.

3. **Industry Adaptation**: Organizations must navigate this
transition thoughtfully. Investing in employee training while
gradually integrating AI solutions can mitigate potential job
losses.

The trajectory suggests a collaborative future where humans and
machines coexist harmoniously. Embracing this evolution could un-
lock unprecedented efficiencies and elevate the customer experience.

Routine Quality Control and Inspection

In an era where precision and efficiency are paramount, the role of AI
in routine quality control and inspection is transformative. Traditionally, quality control involves human inspectors scrutinizing products
for defects, ensuring they meet predefined standards. This manual
process, while effective, is fraught with challenges such as human error, fatigue, and subjectivity.

The Automation Potential in Quality Control

AI's capacity to perform repetitive tasks with unerring accuracy presents a compelling case for its application in quality control. Machines
equipped with computer vision can analyze products at a microscopic
level, detecting flaws that may elude the human eye. For instance:

- **Visual Inspection:** AI-powered cameras can scan thousands of items per minute, identifying defects such as cracks, misalignments, or color discrepancies.

- **Dimensional Measurement:** Laser-based systems measure product dimensions with high precision, ensuring they conform to specifications.

- **Surface Analysis:** AI algorithms detect surface anomalies like scratches or dents on materials.

Real-World Examples of AI in Action

Several industries have already embraced AI-driven quality inspection systems. The automotive sector, for example, employs robots equipped with machine vision to inspect vehicle parts during manufacturing. These robots can spot defects in engine components or body panels much faster than human inspectors.

Electronics manufacturing benefits from AI's ability to inspect printed circuit boards (PCBs). High-resolution cameras paired with deep learning models can identify soldering issues or misplaced components on PCBs, enhancing product reliability.

Food and beverage industries use AI to ensure product consistency and safety. Machine learning models analyze images of food items on production lines, identifying contaminants or irregularities that could compromise quality.

Future Trends in Automated Quality Control

The evolution of AI in quality control doesn't stop at detection. Predictive maintenance is emerging as a significant trend. By analyzing data from sensors embedded in machinery, AI can predict when equipment will fail or require maintenance. This proactive approach minimizes downtime and enhances productivity.

AI-driven inspection systems are also becoming more adaptable. With advancements in machine learning, these systems can learn from new data continuously, improving their accuracy over time. They adapt to changes in product design or manufacturing processes without requiring extensive reprogramming.

Implications for Human Inspectors

While the rise of AI in routine quality control may seem daunting for human inspectors, it opens up new opportunities. Rather than performing repetitive tasks prone to error, inspectors can focus on more complex issues that require human judgment and creativity.

Human workers can assume roles such as:

- **Oversight and Supervision:** Ensuring that AI systems operate correctly and intervening when anomalies arise.

- **Continuous Improvement:** Using insights from AI data to enhance production processes and product design.

- **Maintenance and Troubleshooting:** Keeping sophisticated AI machinery running smoothly.

Case Studies Highlighting Successes

Consider how Airbus has integrated AI into their quality control processes. Using advanced machine vision systems paired with deep learning algorithms, Airbus inspects aircraft components for defects quickly and accurately. This integration has significantly reduced inspection times while maintaining high safety standards.

In consumer electronics, companies like Samsung leverage AI for inspecting smartphone screens. Automated systems detect micro-defects invisible to the naked eye, ensuring only flawless screens reach consumers.

AI's role in routine quality control and inspection exemplifies its transformative potential across various industries. As technology advances, the synergy between human expertise and artificial intelligence will redefine traditional practices—ushering in an era of unprecedented precision and efficiency.

Standardized Report Generation

Standardized report generation is being significantly transformed by advancements in AI technology. In the past, this task required a lot of human effort, including data collection, analysis, and creating coherent reports. Now, AI is starting to change this process by automating many of the repetitive and time-consuming tasks.

Efficiency Through Automation

AI-powered tools can now create reports quickly and accurately. These systems can gather data from different sources, analyze patterns, and present findings in an organized way. The benefits are clear:

- **Time Savings:** AI can process large amounts of data in seconds, a task that would take humans hours or even days.

- **Consistency:** Automated systems ensure that reports follow standardized formats and guidelines without deviation.

- **Accuracy:** By reducing human error, AI improves the reliability of data presented in reports.

Examples of tools that enable these improvements include **Natural Language Generation (NLG)** platforms like *Narrative Science* and *Automated Insights*, which convert data into natural language text.

Applications Across Industries

Standardized report generation is not limited to one industry; it is used in various sectors:

1. **Finance:** Banks and financial institutions use AI to generate regular financial statements, investment summaries, and compliance reports.

2. **Healthcare:** Medical professionals rely on AI-generated reports for patient records, diagnostics summaries, and treatment plans.

3. **Marketing:** Marketing teams utilize AI to compile campaign performance reports, customer insights, and trend analyses.

Case Study: Financial Reporting

Take the example of a multinational company needing quarterly financial statements. Traditionally, this involves multiple teams working across different geographic locations, consolidating data manually—making it prone to inconsistencies. Implementing an AI solution like *KPMG Clara* allows for real-time data integration and report generation. The system ensures uniformity across all branches and significantly reduces the lag between data collection and reporting.

Overcoming Challenges

While the benefits are clear, integrating AI into standardized report generation comes with its own set of challenges:

- **Data Quality:** For AI to generate meaningful reports, the input data must be accurate and well-structured.

- **User Training:** Employees must be trained to effectively use these new tools, ensuring they can interpret AI-generated reports correctly.

- **Initial Costs:** Although cost-effective in the long run, the initial investment in AI technologies can be substantial.

Future Prospects

The future holds even more advanced AI capabilities. Emerging technologies like *Machine Learning (ML)* will enable systems to not only generate static reports but also predict trends and provide actionable insights:

- **Predictive Analytics:** Anticipating future scenarios based on historical data trends.

- **Interactive Reports:** Allowing users to interact with generated reports for deeper insights.

The role of humans will shift from generating these reports to interpreting them—focusing on strategic decision-making rather than routine tasks.

Ethical Considerations

The rise of AI also brings ethical considerations:

- **Transparency:** Ensuring that the processes involved in report generation are transparent.

- **Bias Mitigation:** Addressing potential biases in data sets that could skew results.

Adopting best practices for ethical use will be crucial as organizations increasingly rely on AI for their reporting needs.

The transformation driven by AI in standardized report generation highlights its growing importance across industries. As organizations continue to adopt these technologies, they must navigate both opportunities and challenges to fully harness the potential of automation while upholding ethical standards.

Inventory Management and Stock Keeping

Modern inventory management and stock keeping are dramatically evolving due to AI integration. Traditionally, these tasks required meticulous attention to detail, substantial manual labor, and a significant amount of time. The rise of AI has revolutionized how businesses handle these processes.

Automation in Inventory Management

AI-powered systems excel in inventory management by predicting demand, optimizing stock levels, and reducing waste. Using machine learning algorithms, these systems analyze historical data to forecast future inventory needs accurately. This predictive capability ensures that businesses maintain optimal stock levels, minimizing both over-stocking and stockouts.

Case Study: Amazon's Kiva Robots

Amazon's implementation of Kiva robots exemplifies AI's transformative impact on inventory management. These robots navigate vast warehouses efficiently, retrieving items for shipment with precision. This automation reduces human error, speeds up order processing, and enhances overall efficiency.

Benefits of AI in Stock Keeping

1. **Accuracy**: AI systems reduce human errors in stock keeping by providing real-time updates and automated tracking.

2. **Efficiency**: Tasks that once took hours can be completed in minutes with AI-driven tools.

3. **Cost Savings**: Reduced labor costs and minimized losses from overstocking or stockouts lead to significant financial benefits.

AI Tools Enhancing Inventory Management

Several advanced tools are at the forefront of this transformation:

- **Walmart's Shelf-Scanning Robots**: These robots scan shelves for out-of-stock items and pricing errors, ensuring shelves are always stocked correctly.

- **Zebra Technologies' SmartLens**: This system uses RFID technology to track inventory throughout the supply chain, offering detailed insights into product movement.

Challenges and Considerations

While the benefits of AI in inventory management are undeniable, there are challenges to consider:

- **Initial Investment**: Implementing AI systems requires substantial upfront investment in technology and training.

- **Data Privacy Concerns**: With the extensive data collection involved, businesses must ensure robust data privacy measures.

- **Job Displacement**: As AI takes over routine tasks, there is potential for job displacement among workers traditionally involved in these roles.

Future Trends in AI-Driven Inventory Management

The future holds promising advancements:

- **Integration with IoT (Internet of Things)**: Combining AI with IoT devices will enable real-time monitoring of inventory conditions such as temperature and humidity.

- **Blockchain for Supply Chain Transparency**: Blockchain technology can enhance transparency and traceability in the supply chain when integrated with AI systems.

The advent of AI in inventory management signifies a pivotal shift towards more efficient, accurate, and cost-effective operations within various industries. The continual evolution of these technologies promises even greater advancements on the horizon.

Scheduling and Appointment Setting

Automating Routine Scheduling Tasks

Scheduling and appointment setting, traditionally laborious tasks, are increasingly falling under the domain of artificial intelligence. AI-driven tools excel at managing calendars, booking appointments, and sending reminders. By leveraging natural language processing (NLP) and machine learning algorithms, these tools can interpret user commands and execute tasks efficiently.

Examples of AI Tools for Scheduling:

- **Calendly:** An intelligent scheduling assistant that synchronizes with personal calendars, allowing users to automate the process of finding mutually convenient meeting times.

- **x.ai:** This tool utilizes AI to handle meeting requests via email, coordinating times based on users' availability without human intervention.

Benefits:

- **Efficiency:** AI scheduling tools can process multiple

requests simultaneously, reducing the time spent on back-and-forth communications.

- **Error Reduction:** Automated systems minimize the risk of double-booking or overlooking appointments.

Tools That Automate Communications

AI's ability to handle routine communications extends beyond just scheduling. Tools like chatbots manage follow-up emails, confirmations, and reminders, ensuring consistent communication flow without manual input.

Key Features:

- **Personalization:** Modern AI can tailor messages to individual recipients, enhancing engagement.

- **24/7 Availability:** Unlike human operators, AI-driven systems provide round-the-clock service.

The Future of Administrative Roles in a Tech-Driven Workplace

As AI continues to evolve, the landscape for administrative roles is transforming. Traditional responsibilities are being redefined as machines take over repetitive tasks. This shift offers administrative professionals opportunities to focus on higher-value activities such as strategic planning and relationship management.

Potential Changes:

- **Skillset Evolution:** The demand for technical skills will rise as administrators may need to oversee and manage AI systems.

- **Job Redefinition:** Roles will likely emphasize creative problem-solving and interpersonal skills that machines cannot replicate.

Real-World Examples

Numerous organizations have successfully integrated AI into their scheduling processes:

1. **IBM Watson Assistant:** Deployed in large enterprises for internal meeting coordination, Watson Assistant significantly reduces the administrative workload.

2. **Google Duplex:** This technology exemplifies the future potential by making phone calls to book appointments on behalf of its users, demonstrating seamless human-AI interaction.

Ethical Considerations and Challenges

While the advantages are compelling, incorporating AI into scheduling brings ethical concerns and challenges:

Privacy Issues:

- Automated systems handling sensitive information must adhere to stringent privacy standards to prevent data breaches.

Bias in Algorithmic Decisions:

- Ensuring fairness in scheduling algorithms is crucial to avoid inadvertent discrimination against certain groups or individuals.

The integration of AI into scheduling and appointment setting represents a significant leap forward in workplace efficiency. As these technologies advance, their role will likely expand beyond mere task automation to more sophisticated applications that enhance decision-making processes.

Basic IT Support and Troubleshooting

The world of basic IT support and troubleshooting is changing dramatically because of advancements in artificial intelligence (AI). Traditionally, IT support roles involve diagnosing and fixing technical issues, managing software installations, and providing guidance on using technology. However, AI-driven solutions are increasingly capable of performing these tasks with remarkable efficiency.

Overview of Basic IT Support Tasks

Basic IT support typically encompasses:
- **Diagnosing hardware/software issues**

- **Assisting with software installations and updates**

- **Guiding users through troubleshooting steps**

- **Resetting passwords and managing user accounts**

These tasks, while essential, often follow repetitive patterns that make them prime candidates for automation.

The Role of AI in IT Support

Artificial intelligence systems excel at recognizing patterns and automating processes. In the world of IT support, AI can handle common queries and issues without human intervention. For example:

- **Chatbots**: Virtual assistants can resolve common technical problems by guiding users through step-by-step solutions.

- **Automated diagnostics**: AI tools can scan systems for issues, identify root causes, and suggest or implement fixes.

Examples of AI Tools in IT Support

1. **IBM Watson Assistant**: Deployed by numerous organizations to handle routine queries, Watson Assistant leverages natural language processing to understand user inquiries and provide accurate responses.

2. **Microsoft's Azure AI**: Utilized for predictive maintenance and automated troubleshooting, Azure AI helps preempt technical failures before they become critical.

3. **ServiceNow's Virtual Agent**: Integrates within existing ServiceNow platforms to assist users with common tech issues around the clock.

Benefits of AI in Troubleshooting

Implementing AI in basic IT support offers several advantages:

- **Efficiency**: AI can resolve issues faster than human agents by instantly accessing vast databases of knowledge.

- **Consistency**: Automated systems provide uniform solutions, reducing the variability associated with human troubleshooting.

- **Scalability**: Virtual agents can handle multiple queries simultaneously, allowing companies to scale their support services without proportional increases in staffing.

Future Prospects for IT Support Roles

While AI excels at handling routine tasks, complex problem-solving still requires human finesse. The future landscape will likely see a hybrid approach where:

- **Human agents focus on complex issues**: Tasks requiring nuanced understanding or creative problem-solving will remain within human purview.

- **AI handles routine matters**: Simple troubleshooting steps will be managed by intelligent systems.

This shift allows human IT professionals to engage in more meaningful work that demands higher cognitive skills.

Case Studies Highlighting the Transition

Two notable examples illustrate the transformative impact of AI in basic IT support:

1. **AT&T's Use of Chatbots**: AT&T implemented a chatbot

system capable of handling up to 70% of customer service interactions related to technical support. This reduced wait times significantly and allowed human agents to tackle more intricate problems.

2. **Hewlett-Packard (HP) Enterprise's Predictive Maintenance**: HP utilizes AI-driven predictive maintenance tools that monitor hardware performance continuously. These tools predict potential failures before they occur, minimizing downtime and ensuring seamless operations.

Content Creation and Copywriting

Content creation and copywriting, which have traditionally relied on human creativity and intuition, are increasingly being influenced by advancements in AI. The integration of AI in these fields is changing how content is created, edited, and distributed.

Automation in Content Generation

AI-driven tools like **GPT-4** have shown impressive abilities in producing coherent and contextually relevant text. These tools can generate articles, social media posts, and even creative writing pieces. They analyze large amounts of data to understand context, tone, and style, enabling them to mimic human-like writing.

Example: A marketing agency uses GPT-4 to draft blog posts tailored to different audience segments.

The AI analyzes previous blog performance data to optimize the content for engagement.

Enhancing Copywriting Efficiency

Copywriting involves crafting persuasive text aimed at driving specific actions. AI tools now assist copywriters by:

1. **Generating multiple versions of ad copy** based on target audience insights.

2. **A/B testing variations** to identify the most effective messaging.

3. **Providing real-time feedback** on readability and emotional tone.

Tool Example: **Copy.ai** leverages natural language processing (NLP) to create compelling ad copies, email campaigns, and product descriptions. It saves time for copywriters by offering a foundation they can refine.

Personalized Content at Scale

Personalization is key in modern marketing strategies. AI algorithms analyze user behavior, preferences, and demographics to tailor content accordingly. This level of customization was previously unfeasible due to the sheer volume of data involved.

> *Case Study:* An e-commerce platform employs AI to personalize product recommendations and marketing emails. By analyzing purchase history and browsing patterns, the AI delivers content that resonates with individual users, enhancing engagement and conversion rates.

Challenges and Ethical Considerations

Despite its advantages, AI in content creation poses challenges:

1. **Quality Control:** While AI can generate text rapidly, ensuring it meets high-quality standards requires human oversight.

2. **Authenticity:** Maintaining an authentic brand voice is crucial. Over-reliance on AI might lead to generic or misaligned content.

3. **Ethical Use:** The ease of generating large volumes of content raises concerns about misinformation and plagiarism.

> "AI can augment human creativity but not replace it entirely," says John Smith, a notable expert in digital marketing ethics.

Future Prospects

The trajectory of AI in content creation points towards more advanced capabilities:

- **Adaptive Learning:** Future AI models will continuously
  learn from new data inputs, improving their understanding
  of niche topics.

- **Emotion Detection:** Enhanced NLP will allow AI to better
  gauge emotional nuances in writing, creating more empathetic content.

- **Collaborative Tools:** Integration with collaborative platforms will streamline the workflow between human writers
  and AI assistants.

Hypothetical Scenario: Imagine a virtual newsroom
where journalists collaborate with AI editors that
suggest headlines based on trending topics while
proofreading articles for factual accuracy.

AI's role in content creation and copywriting represents a significant shift in how we approach communication. While it offers
unprecedented efficiency and personalization capabilities, the human
element remains essential for maintaining quality and authenticity. As
technology evolves, finding a balance between automated efficiency
and human creativity will be key in leveraging the full potential of
AI-driven content solutions.

Simple Graphic Design and Photo Editing

AI is changing the world of graphic design and photo editing. Tasks that used to take hours are now being done faster and more efficiently with the help of intelligent algorithms.

Automation in Graphic Design

AI-powered tools like **Canva**, **Adobe Sensei**, and **Designify** are transforming how we approach design. These platforms offer pre-made templates, auto-layout adjustments, and even design suggestions based on user input. By analyzing patterns in design choices, AI can recommend color palettes, typography, and layout arrangements that resonate with target audiences. This not only speeds up the design process but also ensures consistency and quality across different projects.

Examples:

- **Canva**: Provides drag-and-drop features with AI-driven template suggestions.

- **Adobe Sensei**: Enhances Adobe Creative Cloud by offering smart editing tools.

- **Designify**: Utilizes AI to transform simple sketches into polished designs.

Photo Editing Reimagined

In the world of photo editing, AI is making significant advancements. Tools such as **Luminar AI**, **Photoshop Elements**, and **Pixelmator Pro** use machine learning to enhance images automatically. These applications can retouch photos, remove backgrounds, adjust lighting, and even apply artistic filters without requiring advanced skills from the user.

Key Features:

- **Automatic Retouching**: Removes blemishes and smoothens skin tones.

- **Background Removal**: Isolates subjects from their backgrounds seamlessly.

- **Lighting Adjustments**: Balances exposure levels for a professional look.

Impact on Human Roles

The rise of these intelligent tools raises questions about the future role of human designers and editors. While AI handles repetitive tasks efficiently, the essence of creativity—conceptualization, emotional resonance, storytelling—still rests firmly in human hands. AI acts as an enabler rather than a replacer.

Hypothetical Scenario: Imagine a marketing agency where designers use AI to generate initial concepts quickly. They then refine these ideas, infusing them with the brand's unique voice and vision. The result is a harmonious blend of machine efficiency and human creativity.

Future Trends

Looking ahead, the integration of AI in graphic design and photo editing will likely deepen. As algorithms become more sophisticated, they could offer even more nuanced insights into design trends and audience preferences. Collaborative tools that allow real-time feedback between human designers and AI could redefine workflow dynamics.

Prospective Developments:

1. *Real-time Collaboration*: Designers working alongside AI for instant edits.

2. *Predictive Analytics*: Anticipating design trends based on consumer data.

3. *Advanced Customization*: Highly personalized designs tailored to individual tastes.

Ethical Considerations

With increased automation comes ethical concerns about originality and authenticity in creative work. While AI can replicate styles and techniques, it raises questions about intellectual property rights and the value of human artistry.

Quote for Thought:

"Creativity is allowing yourself to make mistakes. Art is knowing which ones to keep." — Scott Adams

Balancing the benefits of automation with maintaining artistic integrity will be crucial as we navigate this evolving landscape.

AI's role in simple graphic design and photo editing illustrates a broader trend towards augmenting human capabilities rather than outright replacement. The challenge lies in harnessing this technology ethically while preserving the unique touch that only humans can provide.

Market Research and Survey Analysis

Market research and survey analysis have long been the backbone of strategic decision-making in businesses. Collecting, analyzing, and interpreting data to understand market trends and consumer behavior requires meticulous attention to detail. This is where AI steps in, streamlining processes that were once labor-intensive and time-consuming.

Automation in Data Collection

Automation in data collection has revolutionized market research. Manual surveys and questionnaires, often fraught with human error and biases, are being replaced by AI-driven tools. For instance, **Natural Language Processing (NLP)** algorithms can analyze open-ended responses more accurately than humans. These tools can sift through vast amounts of text data to identify patterns and sentiments.

> *Example*: **SurveyMonkey** utilizes machine learning to offer predictive insights from survey data, reducing the need for extensive manual analysis.

Enhanced Data Analysis

AI excels at identifying correlations and trends within massive datasets. Traditional methods might overlook subtle but significant patterns due to the sheer volume of data. Machine learning algorithms, however, can process this information efficiently, providing deeper insights into consumer preferences and market dynamics.

> *Tool Highlight*: **IBM Watson Analytics** uses advanced analytics to visualize data trends and generate predictive models, allowing businesses to make informed decisions quickly.

Real-Time Insights

In a fast-paced business environment, timely insights are crucial. AI-powered market research tools provide real-time analytics, enabling companies to respond swiftly to market changes. This capability is transforming how businesses approach marketing strategies and product development.

> *Case Study*: **Coca-Cola** leverages AI for real-time social media monitoring, enabling them to gauge consumer sentiment instantly and adjust their marketing campaigns accordingly.

Survey Design Optimization

Designing effective surveys is critical for obtaining high-quality data. AI aids in optimizing survey questions by analyzing past responses and suggesting improvements. This ensures higher response rates and more reliable data.

> *Example*: **Qualtrics** employs machine learning algorithms to refine survey designs based on previous respondent behavior, enhancing the overall quality of the collected data.

Predictive Analytics

Predictive analytics powered by AI helps businesses forecast future trends based on historical data. This aspect of market research is invaluable for strategic planning, as it allows companies to anticipate shifts in consumer behavior and adjust their strategies proactively.

> *Tool Highlight*: **Google Analytics 360** integrates AI-driven predictive analytics to provide insights into potential future customer actions, aiding businesses in crafting more effective marketing strategies.

Challenges and Ethical Considerations

While AI offers numerous advantages in market research, it also presents challenges. Ensuring data privacy and addressing ethical concerns around algorithmic biases are paramount. Companies must navigate these issues carefully to maintain trust with their customers.

> *Quote*: As Dr. Fei-Fei Li eloquently puts it, "It is a fundamental human right for individuals to own their own data."

Future Prospects

The future of market research lies in the continued integration of AI technologies. As these tools become more sophisticated, they will not only enhance the accuracy of market analysis but also democratize access to high-quality research across industries.

The seamless application of AI in market research exemplifies its transformative potential across various domains. By automating routine tasks and providing actionable insights swiftly, AI paves the way for more strategic decision-making processes in businesses worldwide.

Logistics and Supply Chain Management

Automation in Logistics

Automation has become a cornerstone in transforming logistics and supply chain management. The integration of AI and machine learning algorithms into logistics workflows ensures real-time decision-making, minimizing human error. Autonomous vehicles, drones, and robotic systems are revolutionizing the delivery process by handling tasks traditionally performed by humans.

Key Areas Impacted by AI:

- **Route Optimization:** AI algorithms analyze traffic patterns, weather conditions, and delivery schedules to determine the most efficient routes.

- **Inventory Management:** Automated systems monitor stock levels in real-time, predict demand trends, and trigger re-orders without manual intervention.

- **Warehouse Operations:** Robotics handle picking, packing, and sorting tasks with greater speed and accuracy compared to human labor.

Role of Robotics

Robots have firmly established their place in modern warehouses. They perform repetitive tasks such as lifting and transporting goods, allowing human workers to focus on more complex responsibilities. Collaborative robots (cobots) work alongside humans, enhancing productivity without replacing the need for human oversight.

Examples of Robotics in Warehousing:

- **Automated Guided Vehicles (AGVs):** Transport materials within warehouses autonomously.

- **Robotic Arms:** Execute precise picking and packing operations.

- **Drones:** Conduct inventory checks and manage stock levels efficiently.

Predictive Analytics

AI-driven predictive analytics play a pivotal role in anticipating future trends within supply chains. By analyzing historical data, AI can forecast demand fluctuations and potential disruptions. This proactive approach enables companies to mitigate risks and adapt their strategies accordingly.

Applications of Predictive Analytics:

- **Demand Forecasting:** Predicts customer demand using data from past sales, market trends, and seasonal factors.

- **Risk Management:** Identifies potential supply chain disruptions such as natural disasters or political instability.

- **Maintenance Scheduling:** Predicts equipment failures before they occur, ensuring smooth operations.

Real-life Implementation

Numerous companies have successfully harnessed AI to enhance their logistics processes:

1. **Amazon:** Utilizes a combination of robotics for warehouse automation and sophisticated algorithms for route planning.

2. **DHL:** Employs AI-powered predictive analytics to optimize delivery routes and improve fuel efficiency.

3. **Walmart:** Implements automated systems for inventory

management across its vast network of stores.

Ethical Considerations

While AI offers significant advantages in logistics, it also brings ethical challenges:

- **Job Displacement:** Automating tasks traditionally performed by humans raises concerns about job losses.

- **Privacy Issues:** Real-time tracking and monitoring may infringe on privacy rights.

- **Bias in Algorithms:** Ensuring that AI systems operate fairly without discrimination is crucial.

Mitigation Strategies:

- **Upskilling Workforce:** Investing in training programs to equip employees with skills needed for new roles created by AI advancements.

- **Transparent Policies:** Establishing clear guidelines on data usage to protect privacy.

- **Ethical AI Development:** Implementing standards to ensure fairness in algorithmic decision-making.

Future Trends

The future of logistics lies at the intersection of technology and innovation. Emerging trends point towards even greater reliance on AI:

1. **Blockchain Integration:** Enhances transparency and security within supply chains.

2. **IoT Connectivity:** Facilitates seamless communication between devices for real-time tracking.

3. **Sustainability Initiatives:** AI-driven solutions aim to reduce environmental impact through optimized resource usage.

The integration of artificial intelligence into logistics heralds a new era of efficiency and precision. With ongoing advancements in technology, the landscape will continue to evolve, offering novel solutions that push the boundaries of what's possible in supply chain management.

Standardized Test Grading and Assessment

Standardized test grading is one of the most promising areas for AI intervention. The repetitive nature of grading multiple-choice tests, essays, and other standardized assessments makes it a perfect candidate for automation.

Automation in Grading Processes

Grading standardized tests requires consistency and precision. AI systems are designed for these tasks, providing unmatched accuracy and speed in evaluating student responses. **Optical Character Recognition (OCR)** technology has transformed the grading of multiple-choice questions, allowing machines to scan answer sheets and compare responses against answer keys with minimal error.

How AI is Used in Grading

Here are some ways AI is being used in the grading process:

- **AI Algorithms:** Modern algorithms can analyze written responses, assessing grammar, coherence, and relevance with high reliability.

- **Machine Learning Models:** These models can be trained on large datasets to predict scores that align closely with human graders.

Benefits of AI in Test Assessment

Using AI in test grading offers several benefits beyond just being efficient.

1. **Consistency:** Unlike human graders who can get tired or biased, AI systems treat all assessments the same way.

2. **Speed:** Machines can go through thousands of tests much faster than a human could, which means quicker results.

3. **Cost-Effectiveness:** Having fewer people needed to grade tests can save schools a lot of money.

Real-World Examples

Some organizations have already started using AI in their assessment processes:

- **ETS's e-rater®**: This tool evaluates GRE® essays by an-

alyzing linguistic features such as syntax and semantics. It
provides instant feedback on writing quality.

- **Pearson's Intelligent Essay Assessor (IEA):** Using natural
  language processing (NLP), IEA grades essays by comparing
  them against a database of previously scored samples.

Case Study: Automated Essay Scoring

A significant study done by the University of Akron found that automated essay scoring systems could match human graders' accuracy.
The research looked at over 16,000 student essays graded by both
humans and machines. Results showed a high correlation between the
two sets of scores, confirming the effectiveness of AI in this area.

Future Implications for Educators

The growing use of AI for test grading brings about important
changes in educational roles:

Impact on Teachers

With less time spent on grading tasks, teachers can now prioritize
personalized instruction and actively engage with students.

Impact on Administrators

Streamlined grading processes free up resources for strategic planning
and curriculum development.

Impact on Students

Faster feedback loops enable students to recognize and address learning gaps promptly.

Ethical Considerations

While the benefits are compelling, ethical questions surround the use of AI in education:

- **Bias Mitigation:** Ensuring that AI systems do not perpetuate existing biases present in training data is crucial.

- **Transparency:** Maintaining transparency about how AI algorithms function helps build trust among stakeholders.

AI's role in standardized test grading represents a significant change in education assessment. By improving efficiency, consistency, and cost-effectiveness, these technologies offer substantial benefits while also raising important ethical considerations. This ongoing evolution invites educators to rethink traditional practices and embrace innovative solutions that prioritize both accuracy and fairness in student evaluation.

Current AI Capabilities: Tasks it Does Most Effectively

Artificial Intelligence (AI) has proven its effectiveness in various areas by automating repetitive tasks, improving efficiency, and enabling data-driven decision-making. Below is a summary of AI's current capabilities, highlighting tasks where it excels.

1. Data Entry and Clerical Work

AI's precision and speed make it ideal for data entry tasks. Systems like Optical Character Recognition (OCR) can scan and digitize handwritten or printed documents with remarkable accuracy. For instance, **UiPath** and **Blue Prism** offer robotic process automation (RPA) tools that streamline clerical work, reducing human error and increasing productivity.

2. Customer Service and Support

In customer service, AI chatbots and virtual assistants handle routine inquiries efficiently. According to a report by *Gartner*, by 2022, **70% of customer interactions involved some form of AI technology**, up from 15% in 2018. Tools like **Zendesk's Answer Bot** provide instant support, freeing human agents to tackle more complex issues.

3. Manufacturing and Assembly Line Jobs

AI-driven robotics are changing the game in manufacturing. These robots are equipped with sensors and machine learning algorithms that allow them to perform intricate tasks on assembly lines with consistent precision. A study by the *International Federation of Robotics* noted that **industrial robot installations reached 373,000 units in 2019**, indicating a significant shift towards automation.

4. Retail Sales and Cashier Positions

Retail environments are increasingly adopting AI-driven systems for seamless transactions. Self-checkout kiosks equipped with computer vision reduce wait times while enhancing customer satisfaction. Additionally, virtual assistants like **Amazon's Alexa** provide personalized shopping experiences, impacting traditional cashier roles.

5. Routine Administrative Tasks

Scheduling meetings, managing emails, and organizing files are tasks ripe for AI intervention. Tools such as **Microsoft's Cortana** and **Google Assistant** automate calendar management and communication, allowing administrative professionals to focus on strategic activities.

6. Basic Financial Analysis and Accounting

Financial analysis benefits immensely from AI's analytical capabilities. Machine learning models can analyze vast datasets to identify trends or anomalies more swiftly than humans. Software like **Xero** and **Quick-Books** automate routine accounting tasks such as invoicing and reconciliation, streamlining financial operations.

7. Transportation and Delivery Services

Autonomous vehicles represent a significant leap in transportation technology. Companies like **Waymo** are developing self-driving cars that promise safer roads and reduced delivery times. A *McKinsey* report projects that autonomous vehicles could deliver **80% of all goods within cities by 2030**, showcasing their potential impact.

8. Simple Legal Research and Document Review

Legal research is another area where AI demonstrates its efficiency. Platforms such as **ROSS Intelligence** utilize natural language processing (NLP) to sift through legal documents swiftly, providing relevant information without human intervention. This reduces the workload on paralegals while ensuring thorough document review.

9. Radiology and Basic Medical Diagnostics

Medical diagnostics have seen revolutionary changes with AI integration. Algorithms trained to interpret medical images can detect anomalies quicker than radiologists in some cases. Research published in the *Journal of the American Medical Association* found that an AI system diagnosed breast cancer with an accuracy rate of **94%, surpassing human radiologists' performance**.

10. Telemarketing and Sales Calls

AI-driven sales calls leverage NLP to engage potential customers effectively. Tools like **Conversica** use conversational AI to follow up on leads autonomously, allowing sales teams to focus on closing deals rather than initial outreach.

11. Routine Quality Control and Inspection

In quality control, AI systems equipped with machine vision perform inspections faster than human workers while maintaining high accuracy levels. Industries such as automotive manufacturing use these systems to detect defects early in the production process.

12. Standardized Report Generation

Report generation benefits from AI's ability to compile data into coherent narratives rapidly. Platforms such as **Automated Insights' Wordsmith**

High Paying Jobs That AI Can't Touch

High-paying jobs—those that offer substantial financial compensation, often above the median wage—serve as a key aspiration for many professionals. The allure of such positions extends beyond mere economic security; they often symbolize success, expertise, and influence within a given field.

Artificial Intelligence (AI) has transformed the job market. From *automated customer service* to *predictive analytics*, AI's capabilities grow exponentially each year. This technological advancement leads to significant job automation across various industries, raising concerns about the future employment landscape. Routine tasks and roles with repetitive functions face obsolescence, as machines excel in precision and efficiency.

Yet, certain professions remain resilient against AI encroachment. The importance of **human qualities**—such as empathy, creativity, and complex decision-making—cannot be overstated in sustaining these careers. Emotional intelligence plays a pivotal role in fields like psychology and counseling, where understanding and managing human emotions are paramount. Creativity drives innovation and is essential in artistic and literary endeavors, areas where AI still struggles to replicate the nuanced depth of human imagination.

The complexity of human decision-making also sets us apart from machines. Judges, senior managers, and other high-stakes decision-makers rely on a blend of experience, intuition, and ethical considerations that algorithms cannot easily emulate.

While AI continues to reshape the job market landscape, high-paying jobs resistant to automation underscore the enduring value of inherently human attributes. These roles not only demand specialized knowledge but also hinge on qualities uniquely refined through human experience.

The Rise of AI and Its Implications

Brief History and Current Trends

Artificial intelligence, once a mere figment of science fiction, has evolved into a transformative force reshaping industries worldwide. Initially conceptualized in the mid-20th century, AI's journey from rudimentary algorithms to sophisticated machine learning systems is nothing short of remarkable. Notable milestones include:

- **1950s**: Alan Turing's foundational work on machine learning.

- **1980s**: Emergence of expert systems and neural networks.

- **2000s**: Advent of big data fueling AI advancements.

- **2010s**: Surge in deep learning and natural language processing.

Today, AI technologies like autonomous vehicles, predictive analytics, and voice recognition systems are not only feasible but increasingly commonplace.

Rapid Advancement Leading to Job Automation

The rapid progression of artificial intelligence has ushered in an era where machines can perform tasks once deemed exclusively human. Industries across the spectrum—manufacturing, retail, finance—experience significant job automation. For instance:

- **Manufacturing**: Robotic arms streamline assembly lines, enhancing precision and efficiency.

- **Retail**: Automated checkout systems reduce the need for cashiers.

- **Finance**: Algorithms execute high-frequency trading with unparalleled speed.

This surge in automation transforms the workforce landscape, necessitating a reevaluation of traditional roles.

Necessity for Skill Shifts and Adaptability

As AI takes over routine tasks, the demand for skills that complement technological capabilities becomes paramount. Workers must pivot towards roles requiring advanced cognitive abilities. Key areas include:

- **Analytical Thinking**: Interpreting complex data beyond

the reach of standard algorithms.

- **Technological Literacy**: Understanding AI tools to collaborate effectively with machines.

- **Interpersonal Skills**: Navigating social nuances that machines cannot mimic.

The ability to adapt to these shifts determines one's resilience in an evolving job market.

Fear and Fascination Surrounding Job Displacement

The dual sentiments of fear and fascination often accompany discussions about AI's role in job displacement. On one hand:

> *"Automation anxiety"* grips many workers fearing obsolescence as machines encroach upon their domains.

On the other hand:

> *"Techno-utopianism"* celebrates the potential for AI to liberate humans from mundane tasks, allowing for greater creativity and innovation.

Balancing these perspectives requires acknowledging both the challenges and opportunities presented by AI-driven automation.

Recognizing this duality underscores the importance of preparing for an AI-integrated future while valuing inherently human attributes that remain irreplaceable by technology.

Understanding Human Qualities that Set Us Apart from Machines

Emotional Intelligence in the Workplace

Emotional intelligence (EI) is a cornerstone of human interaction, encompassing the ability to perceive, control, and evaluate emotions. Unlike machines, humans possess an intrinsic capability to empathize, understand social cues, and navigate complex interpersonal dynamics. In a professional setting, EI translates into:

- **Effective teamwork:** Building harmonious relationships and fostering a collaborative environment.

- **Leadership:** Inspiring and motivating teams through understanding and managing emotions.

- **Conflict resolution:** Mediating disputes with sensitivity and fairness.

Daniel Goleman, a leading expert on emotional intelligence, emphasizes its significance:

"In the new economy, emotional intelligence will be one of the critical factors determining success."

AI lacks the nuanced understanding required for authentic emotional connections. This deficiency underscores the enduring value of professions where emotional intelligence is paramount, such as psychology, counseling, and human resources.

Creativity: A Beacon of Human Ingenuity

Creativity stands as a testament to human ingenuity and a stark differentiator from machines. While AI can process vast amounts of data to generate patterns or mimic certain artistic styles, it cannot replicate the spontaneous bursts of original thought that drive true innovation. Creativity manifests in various forms:

- **Artistic endeavors:** Painters like Vincent van Gogh revolutionized art with unique styles that no algorithm could predict.

- **Literary works:** Authors such as J.K. Rowling create intricate worlds and characters that resonate deeply with readers.

- **Technological innovation:** Visionaries like Steve Jobs harness creativity to develop groundbreaking products.

Creativity fuels progress across industries by fostering novel ideas and solutions. The ability to think outside conventional paradigms remains a uniquely human trait that AI struggles to emulate.

The Complexity of Human Decision-Making

Human decision-making processes are intricate and multifaceted, often integrating intuition, ethics, and emotional considerations. Unlike algorithms that rely purely on logic and predefined parameters, humans navigate ambiguity through:

- **Moral judgments:** Deciding what is right or wrong in complex scenarios.

- **Intuitive leaps:** Making quick decisions based on gut feelings rather than just data.

- **Contextual awareness:** Understanding the broader impact of decisions within social or cultural contexts.

Consider legal professionals such as judges who must interpret laws while weighing moral implications and societal norms. Their decisions are not merely binary but are informed by a deep understanding of human nature and societal values.

In senior management roles, leaders make strategic choices that balance short-term gains with long-term vision. Such roles demand foresight and adaptability—qualities inherently challenging for AI to replicate effectively.

Summary Points

- Emotional intelligence fosters essential workplace dynamics like teamwork and leadership.

- Creativity drives innovation in art, literature, technology, and beyond.

- Human decision-making incorporates moral judgments, intuition, and contextual awareness.

These uniquely human qualities—emotional intelligence, creativity, and complex decision-making—create an enduring edge over AI. They shape professions requiring nuanced understanding, innovative thinking, and ethical discernment.

High Paying Jobs Resistant to AI Replacement

Irreplaceable jobs are those that rely on the unique human skills impervious to automation. These professions often require emotional intelligence, creativity, and complex decision-making—qualities that machines find challenging to replicate.

Professions Requiring High Levels of Emotional Intelligence

Psychologists and counselors epitomize roles where emotional intelligence is paramount. The ability to understand, interpret, and respond to human emotions is central to their work.

1. Psychologists

They delve into the intricacies of the human mind, diagnosing mental health conditions, and devising treatment plans tailored to individual needs. Machines lack the nuanced understanding of human experiences necessary for effective psychological care.

2. Counselors

These professionals provide guidance through life's challenges, offering support in a deeply personal manner. The empathetic listening and personalized advice they offer can't be matched by AI, which operates on pre-defined algorithms rather than genuine human connection.

Jobs Demanding Creativity

The realm of art and literature stands as a testament to human ingenuity. *Artists and writers* harness their creative faculties in ways that remain out of reach for AI.

1. Artists

Whether it's painting, sculpture, or performance art, artists create works that evoke emotion and provoke thought. Their originality stems from personal experiences and cultural contexts—elements that AI cannot authentically reproduce.

2. Writers

Crafting compelling narratives requires an understanding of human nature and the ability to weave intricate stories that resonate with readers. From novelists to screenwriters, these professionals shape culture through words, an inherently human endeavor.

Roles Necessitating Complex Decision-Making

At the intersection of law and leadership lie positions demanding sophisticated judgment. *Judges and senior managers* exemplify roles where nuanced decision-making is crucial.

1. Judges

Tasked with interpreting laws and delivering verdicts, judges consider not just legal statutes but also ethical implications and societal norms. Their decisions often hinge on empathy and moral reasoning—qualities beyond the mechanical capabilities of AI.

2. Senior Managers

Leading organizations through dynamic markets requires strategic foresight and adaptability. Senior managers make high-stakes decisions involving risk assessment, resource allocation, and team dynamics. The depth of understanding required extends far beyond algorithmic predictions.

> "Machines are good at pattern recognition but poor at pattern creation." — Gary Kasparov

Through these examples, it becomes evident that certain professions draw upon uniquely human attributes that technology struggles to emulate. Emotional intelligence enables psychologists and counselors to connect on a personal level; creativity propels artists and writers towards innovation; complex decision-making allows judges and senior managers to navigate multifaceted challenges effectively.

In examining these irreplaceable jobs, we observe a common thread: each profession thrives on qualities intrinsic to our humanity. Recognizing this helps us appreciate the enduring relevance of these roles amidst rapid technological advancements.

What to Look for in an AI Resistant Career Field

Finding a career that can withstand the rapid growth of artificial intelligence means looking for qualities that machines have a hard time copying. These qualities include advanced problem-solving skills, emotional understanding, and creativity. Here's a closer look at each quality and why it's important for securing jobs that will last.

Complex Problem-Solving and Critical Thinking

AI is great at analyzing large amounts of data to find patterns and make predictions. But when it comes to complicated problem-solving that requires creative thinking, humans are still needed. Jobs in this area often require:

- **Strategic Thinking:** Jobs like management consultants and financial analysts need people who can understand complex situations, think about different possible outcomes, and come up with new strategies.

- **Engineering and Architecture:** Building infrastructure or creating new technology requires knowledge of complicated factors that AI might not fully understand. Human engineers and architects can come up with innovative solutions while considering practical limitations.

- **Scientific Research:** Being able to form theories, conduct experiments, and critically analyze results is essential. Scientists in fields like biomedicine or environmental science have to deal with difficult ethical issues and unexpected problems that AI can't predict.

Emotional Intelligence and Human Interaction

Human connections are crucial in many jobs where understanding feelings and interacting with others are important. Machines can't truly understand or respond to human emotions. Key professions that value these skills include:

- **Healthcare:** Doctors, nurses, and therapists need more than just medical knowledge; they also need compassion to comfort patients. Being able to empathize is vital for providing good care, accurate diagnoses, and overall healing.

- **Counseling:** Psychologists and social workers help people deal with personal difficulties through empathetic listening and personalized advice. Understanding human behavior requires a level of insight beyond what algorithms can provide.

- **Education:** Teachers support not only academic learning but also emotional growth. Building relationships with students, recognizing their individual needs, and adjusting teaching methods accordingly are inherently human tasks.

Creativity and Innovation

Creativity is one of the most valued traits of humanity—an area where AI still struggles despite its ability to create art or music. Jobs that thrive on originality include:

- **Arts:** Painters, musicians, writers, and other artists incorporate their personal experiences into their work, creating pieces that resonate deeply with humans.

- **Entrepreneurship:** Innovators who start businesses or

come up with new business models rely on thinking outside the box. Entrepreneurs spot gaps in the market, imagine unique solutions, and take calculated risks—a mix of creativity and strategic insight.

- **Marketing:** Creating persuasive stories around products or brands requires an understanding of cultural trends and consumer psychology that AI lacks. Creative directors and content strategists excel by tapping into these human elements.

Identifying Career Resilience

To ensure your career stands strong against automation:

1. Look for roles that involve *complex decision-making*.

2. Focus on positions requiring *human-centric interaction*.

3. Embrace fields where *creativity* is key.

These qualities highlight the importance of being resilient in your career as technology continues to advance in the job market.

The Future Job Market: Embracing the Human Edge in a Tech-Driven World

Advancements in AI technology are bringing about a major change in the job market. As automation and machine learning continue to develop, routine tasks in various industries are increasingly being handed over to intelligent systems. This shift requires us to reassess the skills and roles that will be most important in the future job market.

Future Job Market Trends

The **future job market trends** suggest that there will be a greater focus on skills that are uniquely human and difficult for machines to replicate. Despite the capabilities of AI, certain professions will continue to thrive because they rely on inherent human qualities:

1. Emotional Intelligence

Jobs that require empathy, understanding, and interpersonal skills will always be essential. Healthcare workers, therapists, and those in customer service positions will still be in demand because of their ability to navigate complex human emotions.

2. Creativity

Innovation relies on original thinking and artistic expression. Careers in the arts, design, and creative fields highlight the irreplaceable value of human imagination. While AI can imitate patterns, it lacks the ability to come up with new ideas.

3. Complex Decision-Making

Leadership positions often involve intricate decision-making processes that go beyond what algorithms can handle. Senior managers, judges, and policymakers depend on nuanced judgment shaped by their experiences and understanding of specific situations.

Ray Kurzweil once said, *"The key challenge for humanity is finding our unique role as machines become more capable. "* This idea resonates strongly with current trends. As AI becomes more efficient at handling analytical and repetitive tasks, our advantage lies in our emotional depth, creative abilities, and strategic thinking.

A Synergistic Future

The future job market won't diminish human contributions; instead, it will enhance them by combining technological advancements with our natural strengths. Embracing this change requires flexibility and a commitment to lifelong learning so we can make use of AI's potential while celebrating what makes us inherently human.

Opportunity for Redefinition

A tech-driven world doesn't mean an end to jobs; rather it presents an opportunity for redefining them. By focusing on education and training in areas that utilize emotional intelligence, creativity, and complex decision-making skills we can prepare ourselves for a future where humans coexist peacefully alongside machines.

Jobs and Careers That AI Can't Easily Replace

- **Surgeon** - Requires complex decision-making and manual dexterity that AI can't replicate.

- **Psychiatrist** - Involves deep human interaction and understanding of mental health.

- **Anesthesiologist** - Needs precise real-time adjustments and patient monitoring.

- **Dentist** - Combines technical skill and patient care that AI cannot fully automate.

- **Orthodontist** - Requires personalized treatment plans and manual adjustments.

- **Optometrist** - Involves patient interaction and personalized eye care.

- **Pharmacist** - Requires professional judgment and patient counseling.

- **Veterinarian** - Involves hands-on care and diagnosis of animals.

- **Physician Assistant** - Requires patient interaction and clinical decision-making.

- **Nurse Practitioner** - Involves personalized patient care and health management.

- **Physical Therapist** - Requires tailored treatment plans and hands-on therapy.

- **Occupational Therapist** - Involves customized care plans and patient interaction.

- **Speech-Language Pathologist** - Requires personalized therapy and human interaction.

- **Radiation Therapist** - Involves patient-specific treatment and monitoring.

- **Chiropractor** - Requires manual adjustments and personalized care.

- **Clinical Laboratory Technician** - Involves complex analysis and interpretation of lab results.

- **Biomedical Engineer** - Requires innovative problem-solving and design skills.

- **Environmental Engineer** - Involves complex problem-solving and regulatory compliance.

- **Civil Engineer** - Requires creative design and project management.

- **Aerospace Engineer** - Involves innovative design and testing of aerospace systems.

- **Electrical Engineer** - Requires complex problem-solving and design skills.

- **Mechanical Engineer** - Involves creative design and engineering solutions.

- **Chemical Engineer** - Requires innovative process design and safety management.

- **Software Developer** - Involves creative problem-solving and design of software solutions.

- **Data Scientist** - Requires advanced analytical skills and interpretation of data.

- **Cybersecurity Analyst** - Involves dynamic problem-solving and threat management.

- **Information Systems Manager** - Requires strategic planning and management of IT systems.

- **IT Project Manager** - Involves managing complex projects and human resources.

- **Network Architect** - Requires advanced design and optimization of networks.

- **Database Administrator** - Involves complex database management and security.

- **Market Research Analyst** - Requires human insight into market trends and consumer behavior.

- **Financial Analyst** - Involves complex financial analysis and strategic recommendations.

- **Actuary** - Requires advanced mathematical skills and risk assessment.

- **Personal Financial Advisor** - Involves personalized financial planning and advice.

- **Management Consultant** - Requires human insight into organizational improvement.

- **HR Manager** - Involves managing human resources and complex interpersonal issues.

- **Sales Manager** - Requires human interaction and strategic sales planning.

- **Marketing Manager** - Involves creative strategy and market understanding.

- **Operations Manager** - Requires dynamic problem-solving and process optimization.

- **Construction Manager** - Involves project management and on-site decision-making.

- **Project Manager** - Requires coordination of complex projects and human resources.

- **Real Estate Manager** - Involves personalized client interactions and property management.

- **Public Relations Specialist** - Requires strategic communication and human interaction.

- **Lawyer** - Involves complex legal analysis and client advocacy.

- **Judge** - Requires human judgment and interpretation of the law.

- **Legislator** - Involves human insight and decision-making in policymaking.

- **School Principal** - Requires management of educational staff and student interactions.

- **University Professor** - Involves personalized teaching and academic research.

- **Special Education Teacher** - Requires individualized teaching and student care.

- **Therapist/Counselor** - Involves deep human interaction and personalized therapy.

- **Respiratory Therapist** - Requires patient-specific care and manual respiratory treatments.

- **Dietitian/Nutritionist** - Involves personalized dietary planning and counseling.

- **Art Director** - Requires creative vision and artistic skills.

- **Graphic Designer** - Involves creative design and visual communication.

- **Interior Designer** - Requires personalized design solutions and client interaction.

- **Urban Planner** - Involves complex planning and human-centered design.

- **Archaeologist** - Requires human interpretation of artifacts and historical sites.

- **Historian** - Involves research and interpretation of historical events and documents.

- **Psychologist** - Requires deep understanding of human behavior and mental health.

- **Audiologist** - Involves personalized hearing assessments and treatments.

- **Genetic Counselor** - Requires interpreting genetic information and counseling patients.

- **Sociologist** - Involves studying social behavior and human interactions.

- **Anthropologist** - Requires human-centered research and cultural analysis.

- **Museum Curator** - Involves preserving and interpreting artifacts and artworks.

- **Librarian** - Requires managing information and assisting patrons.

- **Event Planner** - Involves coordinating and personalizing events and gatherings.

- **Chef/Head Cook** - Requires culinary creativity and hands-on food preparation.

- **Sommelier** - Involves expert knowledge of wines and personalized recommendations.

- **Barber/Hairdresser** - Requires personalized hair care and styling.

- **Esthetician** - Involves personalized skincare treatments and client interaction.

- **Jeweler** - Requires manual craftsmanship and creative design.

- **Florist** - Involves creative floral design and personalized arrangements.

- **Fashion Designer** - Requires creative vision and manual garment creation.

- **Furniture Maker** - Involves skilled craftsmanship and personalized designs.

- **Landscape Architect** - Requires creative design and environmental planning.

- **Marine Biologist** - Involves field research and complex data analysis.

- **Forestry Manager** - Requires managing natural resources and environmental planning.

- **Zoologist** - Involves studying animal behavior and ecosystems.

- **Wildlife Biologist** - Requires field research and species conservation efforts.

- **Park Ranger** - Involves managing natural parks and human interaction.

- **Agricultural Scientist** - Requires research and innovation in farming practices.

- **Horticulturist** - Involves plant cultivation and personalized landscaping.

- **Meteorologist** - Requires weather prediction and complex data interpretation.

- **Astronomer** - Involves studying celestial objects and interpreting data.

- **Geologist** - Requires field research and interpretation of geological data.

- **Marine Engineer** - Involves designing and maintaining marine equipment and vessels.

- **Ship Captain** - Requires navigation and management of maritime operations.

- **Air Traffic Controller** - Involves real-time decision-making and managing flight operations.

- **Pilot** - Requires manual flying skills and real-time decision-making.

- **Paramedic** - Involves emergency medical care and patient interaction.

- **Firefighter** - Requires physical skills and real-time decision-making.

- **Police Officer** - Involves law enforcement and complex human interactions.

- **Detective/Criminal Investigator** - Requires solving crimes and human intuition.

- **Correctional Officer** - Involves managing inmate populations and maintaining order.

- **Security Specialist** - Requires real-time threat assessment and management.

- **Emergency Management Director** - Involves planning and responding to emergencies.

- **Speechwriter** - Requires personalized writing and creative communication skills.

- **Public Health Administrator** - Involves managing health programs and community interaction.

- **Nonprofit Manager** - Requires managing nonprofit organizations and human resources.

- **Clergy/Pastor** - Involves spiritual guidance and deep human interaction.

Transitioning to AI-Resistant Jobs

Recognizing and leveraging *transferable skills* is crucial in today's rapidly evolving job market. Transitioning to AI-resistant jobs starts with understanding the value of your existing skills, evaluating your personal strengths, and redeploying them into new and emerging roles. This approach cultivates adaptability and resilience, both essential traits for navigating an uncertain future.

Importance of Recognizing Existing Skills

A significant first step in career transition involves acknowledging the skills you already possess. Whether you're a seasoned professional or just starting, you have a unique set of abilities honed through various experiences.

Key reasons to recognize existing skills:

- **Boosts Confidence:** Understanding your skillset provides a confidence boost, making it easier to tackle new challenges.

- **Saves Time and Effort:** Leveraging what you already know can speed up the learning curve for new roles.

- **Enhances Marketability:** Highlighting diverse competencies can make you more attractive to potential employers.

How to Evaluate Personal Strengths

Evaluating personal strengths requires introspection and honest assessment. This process helps identify which skills are most relevant for AI-resistant jobs.

Methods to evaluate your strengths:

1. **Self-Assessment Tools:**

- Utilize online tools like Myers-Briggs Type Indicator (MBTI) or CliftonStrengths.

- These tools provide insights into your personality traits and how they influence your work style.

1. **Feedback from Peers:**

- Seek feedback from colleagues, mentors, and supervisors.

- Constructive criticism can help pinpoint areas where you excel or need improvement.

1. **Skill Inventory:**

- Create a list of all your skills acquired through education, work experience, and hobbies.

- Categorize them into technical (data analysis, programming) and soft skills (communication, leadership).

1. Reflect on Past Experiences:

- Analyze past projects or tasks where you succeeded.

- Identify common factors that contributed to those successes.

Transitioning Skills to New Roles

Once you've identified your transferable skills, the next step is transitioning them into new roles that are less susceptible to automation.

Strategies for transitioning skills:

- **Mapping Skills to Job Requirements:**

- Research job descriptions for AI-resistant roles.

- Match your skill inventory with the required qualifications.

- **Upskilling and Reskilling:**

- Identify gaps in your current skillset relative to desired roles.

- Enroll in courses or training programs to bridge these gaps.

- **Networking:**

- Connect with professionals in fields you're interested in.

- Attend industry events or join relevant online communities to gain insights and opportunities.

- **Practical Application:**

- Apply transferable skills in freelance projects, internships, or volunteer positions.

- Real-world application solidifies your abilities and adds credibility to your resume.

Example: If you are proficient in project management within a traditional manufacturing setting, these skills can be transferred to manage AI integration projects. Your knowledge of workflow optimization, team coordination, and budget management remains valuable while learning new technical aspects of AI technologies.

Identifying transferable skills is an empowering process that allows you to adapt to shifting job markets without starting from scratch. By recognizing what you already bring to the table, evaluating personal strengths through various methods, and strategically transitioning those skills into new roles, you set the foundation for sustainable career growth amidst the rise of AI and automation.

Building a Personalized Learning Plan

Creating a personalized learning plan is essential for navigating the evolving job market. A well-structured learning roadmap helps you align your skills with career objectives, making sure you stay on track and adjust plans as needed.

Steps to Create a Tailored Learning Roadmap

1. Self-Assessment:

- Begin by evaluating your current skill set. Identify strengths and areas for improvement.

- Tools like SWOT analysis (Strengths, Weaknesses, Opportunities, Threats) can be very useful in this stage.

2. Goal Setting:

- Set clear, achievable goals. Break these down into short-term and long-term objectives.

- Use the SMART criteria: Specific, Measurable, Achievable, Relevant, Time-bound.

3. Research and Resources:

- Identify resources that align with your goals. This might include online courses, workshops, books, or mentorship opportunities.

- Platforms like Coursera, Udemy, and LinkedIn Learning offer courses tailored to various skill levels and industries.

4. Create a Timeline:

- Develop a timeline that outlines when you aim to complete each goal.

- Be realistic about the time commitment required for each learning activity.

5. Implement and Reflect:

- Start working on your learning plan. Regularly reflect on what you've learned and how it applies to your career goals.

- Maintain a journal or digital log to track progress and insights.

Aligning Skills with Career Objectives

Aligning your skills with career objectives ensures that your efforts are directed towards meaningful outcomes.

Identify Industry Trends:

Stay updated with industry trends to understand which skills are in demand. Tools like Google Trends and industry-specific reports can provide valuable insights.

Match Skills with Job Requirements:

Analyze job descriptions in your desired field to identify common requirements. Highlight skills that overlap with these requirements in your learning plan.

Seek Feedback:

Regularly seek feedback from peers, mentors, or industry professionals to ensure you're on the right track.

Tracking Progress and Adjusting Plans

Monitoring progress is crucial for staying motivated and making necessary adjustments.

Regular Check-ins:

Schedule regular check-ins (monthly or quarterly) to assess progress against your goals.

Use Tools for Tracking:

Project management tools like Trello or Asana can help you keep track of tasks and deadlines.

Adjust as Needed:

Be flexible and willing to adjust your plan based on new information or unforeseen challenges.

Examples of Practical Implementation

To illustrate the importance of a personalized learning plan:

Jane is an aspiring data analyst who wants to transition from her current role in customer service.

1. *She starts by conducting a self-assessment using a SWOT analysis.*

2. *Jane sets SMART goals such as completing an introductory course on data analytics within three months.*

3. *She identifies resources including Coursera's Data Science specialization and books recommended by industry experts.*

4. *Jane creates a timeline mapping out weekly study hours and key milestones.*

5. *As she progresses through her courses, she maintains a journal documenting her learnings.*

By following these steps, Jane effectively aligns her new skills with her career objectives in data analytics while tracking her progress diligently.

A personalized learning plan serves as a strategic roadmap guiding you through the complexities of skill acquisition in an AI-resistant job market. By taking proactive steps in goal setting, aligning skills with career objectives, and consistently tracking progress, you position yourself for sustained success amidst rapid technological advancements.

Importance of Critical Thinking and Problem Solving in AI-Resistant Jobs

Role in AI-Resistant Jobs

AI-resistant jobs often require a high degree of **critical thinking** and **problem-solving** skills. Unlike routine tasks that can be automated, roles necessitating these skills involve complex decision-making, creativity, and the ability to analyze information from various perspectives. For instance:

- **Healthcare**: Diagnosing patients requires synthesizing symptoms, medical history, and test results, a task demanding deep analytical skills.

- **Education:** Teaching involves not just imparting knowledge but also understanding diverse learning styles and adapting teaching methods accordingly.

- **Management:** Leaders must navigate complex organizational dynamics, make strategic decisions, and solve unique problems that arise.

Techniques to Enhance These Skills

Enhancing critical thinking and problem-solving abilities is essential for staying relevant in an AI-driven economy. Here are some practical techniques:

1. **Practice Analytical Thinking:**

- Engage in activities that require analysis such as puzzles, strategy games, or reading complex texts.

- Regularly question assumptions and evaluate evidence in daily decision-making.

1. **Embrace Reflective Practices:**

- Keep a journal to reflect on decisions made throughout the day.

- Analyze outcomes to understand what worked well and what could be improved.

1. **Seek Diverse Perspectives:**

- Engage in discussions with individuals from different backgrounds.

- Participate in forums or groups that challenge your viewpoints.

1. **Continuous Learning**:

- Enroll in courses focused on critical thinking or problem-solving.

- Attend workshops or seminars that provide practical exercises and real-world scenarios.

1. **Simulation Exercises**:

- Use role-playing scenarios to practice problem-solving in a controlled environment.

- Engage in case studies related to your field of work.

Real-World Applications in Various Industries

Critical thinking and problem-solving are not confined to any single industry but are vital across various sectors:

- **Technology**: Software developers must troubleshoot code issues, optimize algorithms, and innovate new solutions.

- **Finance**: Analysts need to interpret market trends, assess risks, and provide strategic investment advice.

- **Engineering**: Engineers solve technical challenges by designing systems or products that meet specific requirements while considering constraints like cost, safety, and sustainability.

- **Law**: Lawyers analyze legal texts, build cases based on evidence, and develop strategies for litigation or negotiations.

Applying these skills effectively often leads to enhanced job performance and better career prospects. For example:

1. **In Marketing**, professionals use critical thinking to devise campaigns that resonate with target audiences by analyzing consumer behavior data.

2. **In Healthcare**, medical professionals diagnose diseases by evaluating a multitude of patient data points critically rather than relying solely on automated diagnostic tools.

3. **In Education**, teachers who apply problem-solving techniques can create adaptive learning environments that cater to varying student needs.

By focusing on enhancing critical thinking and problem-solving capabilities through targeted techniques and recognizing their application across industries, you can build a resilient career path less susceptible to automation threats.

Developing Emotional Intelligence and Empathy for Future Workplaces

Emotional intelligence and **empathy** are crucial in the changing job market. As machines take over more technical jobs, the importance of *people skills* grows, making these qualities essential in roles that can't be replaced by AI.

Why Emotional Intelligence Matters in the Future Workplace

In a future where technology is everywhere, emotional intelligence (EI) becomes a key factor that sets people apart. Unlike specific skills that can be automated or outsourced, EI includes:

- **Self-awareness**: Knowing your own feelings and how they influence your behavior.

- **Self-regulation**: Controlling your emotions in healthy ways.

- **Motivation**: Being driven to achieve for its own sake.

- **Empathy**: Understanding other people's feelings.

- **Social skills**: Managing relationships to guide others in desired directions.

The Role of Empathy in Professional Settings

Empathy, an essential part of EI, improves communication and teamwork. It allows professionals to connect on a personal level, building trust and collaboration—qualities that robots can't imitate.

How to Improve Your Emotional Intelligence and Empathy Skills

Improving emotional intelligence and empathy takes regular practice. Here are some effective strategies:

1. Practice Self-Reflection

Regularly assess your emotional responses.
Keeping a journal can help you track what triggers your emotions and how you react to them.

2. Engage in Mindfulness Practices

Participate in activities like meditation or yoga to boost self-awareness.
Deep-breathing exercises can also be helpful for managing stress.

3. Master Active Listening Techniques

Pay full attention to the speaker without planning your response.
Summarizing what was said shows that you understand their point of view.

4. Seek Constructive Feedback

Ask colleagues and supervisors for feedback on your interactions.
Use this input to enhance your interpersonal skills.

5. Participate in Empathy Exercises

During conversations, try to see things from others' perspectives.
Volunteering for roles that involve direct contact with diverse groups can also improve your empathy.

The Positive Effects of Emotional Intelligence on Teamwork

High levels of emotional intelligence and empathy have a significant impact on teamwork:

- **Better Communication**: Teams with strong EI communicate more effectively, reducing misunderstandings and conflicts.

- **Greater Trust**: Empathetic team members build stronger bonds, creating an environment where ideas can be freely shared.

- **Improved Conflict Resolution**: Emotionally intelligent individuals are skilled at resolving conflicts by understanding different viewpoints and finding common ground.

- **Higher Morale**: Teams led by emotionally intelligent leaders often have higher morale, leading to increased productivity and job satisfaction.

Example: A tech startup included EI training in their onboarding process. New hires participated in workshops focused on empathy, active listening, and conflict resolution. As a result, they saw better teamwork, lower turnover rates, and increased innovation due to improved collaboration.

In today's fast-changing workplace influenced by AI advancements, developing emotional intelligence and empathy isn't just beneficial; it's necessary. These skills not only protect against automation but also enhance professional relationships, driving success across various industries.

Acquiring Advanced Technical Skills to Stay Relevant in the Job Market

Key Areas of Focus for Future Jobs

In a job market increasingly influenced by automation and artificial intelligence, certain technical skills become not just advantageous but essential. **Data analysis** and **coding** stand out as pivotal competencies.

1. Data Analysis

The ability to interpret and analyze data is crucial across various sectors. Proficiency in tools like Python, R, and SQL can significantly enhance your employability. Understanding data visualization tools such as Tableau or Power BI enables you to present data insights effectively.

2. Coding

Coding skills transcend traditional IT roles. Knowledge of programming languages such as Python, JavaScript, or C++ is increasingly relevant in fields ranging from web development to machine learning.

Resources for Skill Acquisition

You have several options for acquiring these technical skills. Online platforms provide flexible and often affordable learning opportunities.

1. Online Courses

Websites like Coursera, edX, and Udacity offer courses in data analysis and coding with certification options. These platforms often partner with universities and industry leaders to ensure the content is up-to-date and relevant.

2. Coding Bootcamps

Intensive coding bootcamps such as General Assembly, Flatiron School, or Le Wagon are designed to equip you with the necessary skills within a few months. These programs are particularly beneficial if you're looking for a career switch or need to upskill quickly.

3. Self-paced Learning

For those who prefer self-directed learning, resources such as freeCodeCamp, Khan Academy, and Codecademy provide comprehensive tutorials and exercises that allow you to learn at your own pace.

Balancing Technical and Soft Skills

While technical skills are critical, balancing them with soft skills is equally important. Employers value candidates who can combine their technical expertise with strong communication, teamwork, and problem-solving abilities.

Communication Skills

Being able to explain complex technical concepts in simple terms is invaluable. This skill ensures that you can collaborate effectively with non-technical team members.

Teamwork

Working on projects often requires collaboration. Developing interpersonal skills helps in building strong professional relationships.

Problem Solving

The ability to tackle challenges creatively and efficiently is highly sought after. It involves critical thinking and adaptability—qualities that complement your technical skillset.

Investing time in both technical proficiency and soft skill development makes you a well-rounded candidate capable of thriving in an AI-resistant job market. This holistic approach ensures that you remain adaptable and valuable despite technological advancements.

Pursuing Relevant Degrees and Certifications for Career Advancement

Value of Formal Education vs. Certifications in Today's Job Market

In today's fast-changing job market, it's important to understand the difference between formal education and certifications. Traditional degrees, like bachelor's and master's programs, offer a comprehensive curriculum that provides in-depth knowledge and a well-rounded skill set. They often include foundational theories, practical applications, and opportunities for research and internships.

Advantages of Formal Education:

- **Broad Knowledge Base:** Degrees cover extensive subject matter, providing you with a wide-ranging understanding of your field.

- **Networking Opportunities:** Universities often have strong alumni networks and connections with industries.

- **Credibility:** A degree from a reputable institution can add significant value to your resume.

However, certifications offer targeted expertise in specific areas, making them particularly valuable in tech-driven fields where specialized skills are in high demand.

Advantages of Certifications:

- **Focused Learning:** Certifications concentrate on particular skills or technologies, allowing you to become proficient quickly.

- **Cost-Effective:** Often more affordable than a full degree program.

- **Time-Efficient:** Many certification courses can be completed in months rather than years.

Popular Certification Programs in Demand

Several certification programs stand out due to their relevance and recognition in the industry. Here are two prominent examples:

- **AWS Certified Solutions Architect:** *Purpose:* This certification is designed for individuals who want to demonstrate their expertise in designing and deploying scalable systems on Amazon Web Services (AWS).

- *Benefits:* AWS certifications are highly regarded as AWS is a leading cloud service provider. It validates your ability to build secure and robust applications on the AWS platform.

- **Google Data Analytics Professional Certificate:** *Purpose:* Aimed at those looking to break into data analytics, this certification covers essential skills like data cleaning, analysis, visualization, and using tools such as SQL and R.

- *Benefits:* The course is developed by Google and provides practical experience through hands-on projects. It's also accessible via Coursera, making it widely available.

Choosing the Right Educational Path Based on Career Goals

Selecting between degrees and certifications depends significantly on your career aspirations and current position within your professional journey.

Factors to Consider:

- **Career Stage:** If you're just starting out or planning a significant career shift, a degree might provide the comprehensive foundation you need.

- If you're looking to enhance specific skills or pivot within your current field, certifications can offer quick, targeted learning.

- **Industry Requirements:** Certain industries or roles may require formal education credentials. For instance, engineering or healthcare often necessitates accredited degrees.

- Tech roles in areas like cybersecurity or cloud computing might prioritize up-to-date certifications over traditional degrees due to the fast-paced nature of technological advancements.

- **Learning Style and Resources:** Consider whether you prefer structured academic environments or self-paced online learning.

- Evaluate your budget and time constraints—degrees typically require more significant investments of both compared to certifications.

Example Pathways:

- *Aspiring Data Scientist:* You might pursue a bachelor's degree in Computer Science followed by specialized certifications such as IBM Data Science Professional Certificate.

- *Experienced IT Professional Seeking Cloud Expertise:*Opt for targeted certifications like AWS Certified Solutions Architect without necessarily pursuing another degree.

Both degrees and certifications play pivotal roles in career advancement. The key lies in aligning your choice with your long-term career objectives, industry demands, and personal circumstances. Balancing these elements will help you navigate your educational journey effectively while staying competitive in the job market.

Gaining Experience through Internships and Volunteering Opportunities to Boost Employability

Benefits of Real-World Experience in Job Readiness

Practical experience is invaluable when preparing for AI-resistant jobs. Internships and volunteering provide you with hands-on knowledge that can't be obtained through textbooks or online courses alone. These experiences help you:

- **Develop practical skills**: Engaging in real-world tasks allows you to apply theoretical knowledge, enhancing your problem-solving abilities and technical competencies.

- **Understand workplace dynamics**: You'll gain insights into how teams collaborate, the importance of communication, and the workflow within different industries.

- **Build confidence**: Tackling real challenges boosts your confidence and prepares you for future job roles.

- **Enhance your resume**: Employers value candidates who have demonstrated their capabilities in a professional setting. Internships and volunteer work make your resume stand out.

Finding Opportunities That Align with Career Goals

Identifying internships or volunteer positions that match your career aspirations is crucial. Here are some strategies to help you find the right opportunities:

1. **Research companies and organizations**:

- Look for tech startups if you're interested in innovative environments.

- Consider non-profit organizations if you want to contribute to social causes while gaining experience.

1. **Utilize online platforms**:

- Websites like LinkedIn, Glassdoor, and Indeed often list internship opportunities.

- Platforms such as VolunteerMatch can connect you with volunteer positions based on your interests.

1. **Network within your industry**:

- Attend industry events, webinars, or workshops to meet professionals who can offer guidance or recommend openings.

- Join online forums or social media groups related to your field.

1. **Leverage academic resources:**

- Many universities have career services that assist students in finding internships and volunteer work.

- Faculty members can also provide recommendations based on their industry connections.

Networking Through Experiential Learning

Internships and volunteering are not just about gaining experience; they are also powerful networking tools. Building relationships during these periods can open doors for future job opportunities. Here's how experiential learning aids networking:

- **Establishing professional connections:** Working alongside seasoned professionals gives you access to a network of individuals who can mentor you or refer you to job openings.

- **Demonstrating your capabilities:** Your performance during internships or volunteer work serves as a live demonstration of your skills to potential employers.

- **Receiving personalized feedback:** Constructive criticism from supervisors helps you understand areas of improvement and strengths, making you more marketable.

Engage actively with colleagues by participating in team meetings, company events, and social gatherings. This proactive approach helps cement professional relationships that could be beneficial long-term.

Networking and Building Professional Associations for Career Growth

Importance of Building a Professional Network Early On in Your Career Journey

Networking is a crucial element for career advancement, especially in an AI-driven job market. Establishing a professional network early on can significantly impact your career trajectory by providing access to job opportunities, industry insights, and mentorship.

Key Benefits of Early Networking:

- **Access to Hidden Job Markets:** Many positions are filled through referrals or internal recommendations. A strong network increases your chances of learning about these opportunities.

- **Mentorship and Guidance:** Experienced professionals can offer valuable advice, share their experiences, and provide guidance on navigating your career path.

- **Industry Insights:** Staying connected with industry peers keeps you informed about the latest trends, innovations, and best practices.

Effective Networking Strategies for Young Professionals

Building a robust professional network requires deliberate effort and strategic planning. Here are some effective strategies to consider:

- **Attend Industry Events:** Conferences, seminars, and workshops are excellent venues to meet professionals from your field.

- Engage in conversations, exchange business cards, and follow up with new contacts.

- **Utilize LinkedIn:** Create a compelling LinkedIn profile that highlights your skills, experience, and career goals.

- Join relevant industry groups and participate in discussions to showcase your knowledge.

- Connect with professionals you meet at events or through mutual acquaintances.

- **Join Professional Associations:** Becoming a member of organizations like IEEE (Institute of Electrical and Electronics Engineers) or PMI (Project Management Institute) provides access to exclusive networking events, resources, and certifications.

- **Leverage Social Media:** Follow thought leaders and companies on platforms like Twitter to stay updated with industry news.

- Participate in Twitter chats or LinkedIn discussions to connect with like-minded professionals.

- **Engage in Informational Interviews:**Reach out to professionals in roles or companies you're interested in and request informational interviews.

- Use these meetings to gain insights into their career paths, challenges they face, and advice for breaking into the industry.

Leveraging Associations Like IEEE or PMI for Growth Opportunities

Professional associations play a vital role in career development by offering numerous growth opportunities:

Membership Benefits:

- **Exclusive Access to Resources:** Members often receive access to journals, white papers, research reports, and other valuable resources that can enhance their knowledge base.

- **Networking Events:** Associations frequently organize conferences, workshops, webinars, and local chapter meetings. These events provide opportunities to meet industry leaders and peers.

- **Certifications:** Many associations offer certification programs that are recognized globally. For instance:

- *IEEE:* Offers certifications such as Certified Biometrics Professional (CBP) which validate expertise in specialized fields.

- *PMI:* Provides the Project Management Professional (PMP) certification which is highly regarded across industries.

Career Services:

- **Job Boards:** Many associations have dedicated job boards where members can find listings tailored to their field.

- **Mentorship Programs:** Some organizations offer formal mentorship programs connecting seasoned professionals with newcomers.

Community Engagement:

- Joining committees or volunteer groups within the association allows you to contribute actively while expanding your network.

- Writing articles for association publications or speaking at events can position you as a thought leader in your area of expertise.

Networking is not just about collecting contacts but building meaningful relationships that foster mutual growth. By strategically engaging with professional associations and leveraging various networking platforms early on in your career journey, you lay a robust foundation for long-term success.

Staying Updated with Industry Trends to Remain Competitive

Understanding *industry trends* and technological advancements is crucial in today's rapidly changing job market. Keeping yourself updated through *continuous learning* ensures that you remain competitive and adaptable.

Continuous Learning Methods

1. **Online Courses**: Platforms like Coursera, edX, and Udacity offer a plethora of courses on emerging technologies and industry-specific skills. These platforms provide flexibility, allowing you to learn at your own pace.

2. **Webinars**: Attending webinars hosted by industry experts or professional organizations can provide insights into the latest trends and innovations. Websites like Eventbrite or Meetup often list relevant webinars.

3. **Workshops and Bootcamps**: Participating in workshops or bootcamps offers hands-on experience with new tools and methodologies. For example, General Assembly provides intensive bootcamps on coding, data analysis, and more.

Tools for Tracking Trends

Staying updated with industry trends requires utilizing various tools and resources effectively:

- **Industry Newsletters**: Subscribing to newsletters from leading industry publications such as TechCrunch, Wired, or Harvard Business Review can keep you informed about the latest developments.

- **Social Media**: Following thought leaders on platforms like LinkedIn or Twitter enables real-time updates and insights. Thought leaders often share articles, opinions, and research findings that highlight emerging trends.

- **Industry Reports**: Regularly reviewing reports from consulting firms like McKinsey & Company or Deloitte can provide comprehensive analyses of market shifts and future projections.

Practical Applications

Tracking industry trends isn't just about staying informed; it involves applying this knowledge practically:

- **Adapting Skills to Market Demand**: By understanding which skills are becoming more valuable, you can tailor your learning efforts accordingly. For instance, if data analysis is gaining prominence in your field, investing time in mastering tools like SQL or Python could be beneficial.

- **Innovative Solutions**: Awareness of current trends can spark innovative ideas for solving problems within your organization. This proactivity can set you apart as a forward-thinking employee.

Examples of Industry Trends

Several key trends are transforming various industries:

- **Automation and AI**: The integration of AI in business processes is reshaping job roles across sectors. Staying updated on AI applications can help you identify opportunities for implementing these technologies in your work.

- **Remote Work Technologies**: As remote work becomes

more prevalent, understanding tools like Zoom, Slack, and project management software such as Asana is essential for maintaining productivity.

Leveraging Professional Networks

Engage actively with your professional network to gain diverse perspectives on industry trends:

> "Networking isn't just about connecting people. It's about connecting people with ideas and insights." – Michele Jennae

By discussing recent developments with colleagues or mentors, you can gain deeper insights into how these changes might affect your specific career path.

Remaining competitive in an ever-evolving job market necessitates a commitment to continuous learning and proactive engagement with emerging trends. Utilizing online courses, subscribing to newsletters, following thought leaders, and engaging in professional networks are all effective strategies for staying ahead.

Emphasizing Creativity and Innovation as Key Differentiators

How Creative Thinking Complements AI Technologies

Artificial intelligence excels at processing large amounts of data, identifying patterns, and performing repetitive tasks efficiently. However, it lacks the intrinsic human ability to think creatively and innovatively. This is where your unique contributions come into play. Creativity involves generating new ideas, thinking outside the box, and approaching problems from novel angles—capabilities that AI cannot replicate.

The Role of Creative Thinking in Different Areas

1. **Problem-Solving:** While AI can provide data-driven insights, human creativity is essential in interpreting these insights and applying them in ways that drive innovation.

2. **Adaptability:** Creative thinking allows you to adapt quickly to changing environments. In contrast, AI systems often require significant reprogramming to handle new situations.

3. **Emotional Resonance:** Creative work often resonates on an emotional level with people. For instance, art, literature, and original content creation involve nuances that AI struggles to emulate.

Encouraging Innovative Approaches in the Workplace

Fostering a culture of innovation within your organization can lead to groundbreaking solutions and keep you competitive in an AI-driven landscape. Here are some practical strategies:

Brainstorming Sessions

Organize regular brainstorming sessions where team members can freely share ideas without fear of judgment. These sessions should encourage out-of-the-box thinking and consider unconventional solutions.

> *Example:* Google's "20% time" policy allows employees to spend 20% of their time working on projects they are passionate about. This has led to innovations like Gmail and Google News.

Hackathons

Hackathons create a dynamic environment for rapid prototyping and problem-solving. These events bring together diverse teams to work on specific challenges over a short period, fostering creativity through collaboration.

> *Example:* Many tech companies host internal hackathons where employees can develop new products or features. Facebook's Like button originated from one such hackathon.

Innovation Labs

Setting up dedicated innovation labs within your organization can provide a structured yet flexible space for experimenting with new ideas. These labs often have access to advanced tools and technologies that facilitate creative experimentation.

> *Example:* IBM's Watson IoT Center in Munich offers innovators a collaborative space equipped with cutting-edge technology for developing IoT solutions.

Encouraging a Creative Mindset

Developing a creative mindset requires ongoing effort and commitment. Here's how you can cultivate this quality:

- **Curiosity:** Maintain an inquisitive attitude by asking questions and seeking out new experiences. Curiosity drives discovery and fuels innovative thinking.

- **Risk-Taking:** Don't be afraid to take risks or make mistakes. Failure is often a stepping stone to breakthrough innovations.

- **Collaboration:** Engage with colleagues from different departments or industries. Diverse perspectives can lead to unexpected insights and creative solutions.

Real-world Applications

Creativity and innovation are not limited to any single industry; they are universally applicable across various fields.

- **Healthcare:** Innovations like telemedicine platforms have

revolutionized patient care by integrating creative problem-solving with technological advancements.

- **Education:** Interactive learning tools and gamified educational apps leverage creativity to enhance student engagement.

- **Marketing:** Creative campaigns that use storytelling or viral
content effectively capture audience attention in ways standard AI algorithms cannot achieve.

In an era dominated by AI technologies, your ability to think
creatively will set you apart. By encouraging innovative approaches
through brainstorming sessions, hackathons, and fostering a creative
mindset, you contribute unique value that machines cannot replace.
Embrace these strategies to ensure your skills remain relevant and
indispensable in the evolving job market.

www.ingramcontent.com/pod-product-compliance
Lightning Source LLC
LaVergne TN
LVHW022348060326
832902LV00022B/4308